THE VEGETARIAN LUNCHBOX

A collection of delicious and exciting ideas for making the most of lunch using fresh and natural ingredients.

By the same author
COMPASSIONATE GOURMET
FAST AND EASY VEGETARIAN COOKING
THE HOLISTIC COOK
ITALIAN DISHES
NATURAL SWEETS
PIZZAS AND PANCAKES
QUICHES AND FLANS
365+1 VEGETARIAN MAIN MEALS
A VEGETARIAN IN THE FAMILY
VEGETARIAN PASTA DISHES
VEGETARIAN PÂTÉS AND DIPS
VEGETARIAN SNACKS AND STARTERS
THE VERY BEST OF VEGETARIAN COOKING
WHOLEFOOD SWEETS BOOK

THE VEGETARIAN LUNCHBOX

Nutritious Packed Lunches and Hot Snacks

by

Janet Hunt

THORSONS PUBLISHING GROUP
Wellingborough, Northamptonshire

·

Rochester, Vermont

First published 1979 as *The Wholefood Lunch Box*
This edition first published 1986

2   4   6   8   10   9   7   5   3

British Library Cataloguing in Publication Data

Hunt, Janet, *1942-*
   The vegetarian lunchbox: nutritious packed
   lunches and hot snacks. — New ed.
   1. Vegetarian cookery   2. Cookery (Natural
   foods)
   I. Title   II. Hunt, Janet, *1942-* Wholefood
   lunchbox
   641.5'636   TX837

   ISBN 0-7225-1409-3

Printed and bound in Great Britain

CONTENTS

LUNCH: THE NEGLECTED MEAL

Sunday lunch is something of an occasion in most homes. But during the week, lunch is rarely more than a snatched snack at best, a chocolate bar or pint of beer at worst. Most workers prefer to spend their short, precious lunch breaks shopping, writing letters, chatting — anything but eating! For many school children, lunchtime means little more than a chance to get away from school books and watching eyes. As for the housewife — she is always far too busy to worry about eating!

Neglecting lunch is not a universal custom. In many parts of the world, particularly in hotter climates, lunch is treated as a necessary, pleasant and refreshing event. Time is taken to savour the tastes of good, nutritious food — and to digest it, too. And after what might seem like an indulgently long lunch break, work is resumed with the kind of energy and enthusiasm rarely found amongst Britain's workforce (except at clocking-off time).

The Benefits of a Break
In fact, lunch is an important meal, both physically and psychologically. Few people have time to prepare and eat a good breakfast, particularly during the week; yet without it, your energy level will be flagging by midday. To recharge the batteries that will keep you active and alert through the afternoon, your body needs nourishing with a light but wholesome meal. If you can relax whilst eating, and for a short time afterwards, so much the better: not only will your food be assimilated into your system with the minimum of effort, but you'll feel that you have had a complete break.

What you eat is, of course, very relevant too. Restaurant or canteen lunches are fine if you have the facilities and finances necessary. Packed lunches are a better idea, because they mean you can control exactly what you eat, how much it costs, and even where you eat it — on a hot, sunny day, a crowded restaurant cannot compete with a park bench! Packed lunches, however, tend to mean sandwiches. And sandwiches made from refined white bread spread thick with butter, meat pastes or other processed spreads, supply you with a surplus of calories, and not much more.

If you are the one who puts your packed lunch together, you can choose to take nutritious, wholesome foods rather than the empty, calorie-laden kind; you can add variety to your midday snacks with a whole range of foods not often associated with packed lunches, but easy to prepare and tasty to eat (for instance, flans, pizzas, salads, croquettes, cold cooked vegetables); you can make your lunch filling on a cold day, refreshing in the summer, or whatever you fancy.

The aim of this book is to help you produce inexpensive, interesting packed lunches for yourself, your family, or even to share with workfriends. It also has some ideas for the housewife who, by not bothering with lunch, is also neglecting her health, her looks, and her vitality! Most of the recipes are simple and adaptable. Wholesome ingredients are the key to happy lunching — if you remember to use only fresh, unadulterated foods whenever possible, you will not go far wrong.

Ingredients
When looking through this book, you may notice that certain ingredients are conspicuous by their absence. White bread and flour are not recommended for regular use as part of your packed lunches as much of their goodness has been refined out of them, together with the roughage (fibre) that is now being recognized as so vital to health. Certainly you can use them every now and again, but once you are used to the more nutty flavour of real wholewheat bread, it is quite likely that you will find white bread by comparison, soft and unsatisfying.

In most recipes butter has been replaced by margarine, and it is suggested that you use one of the varieties that is low in cholesterol, high in polyunsaturates. This would also be preferable when making sandwiches. Butter certainly has nutritional value, but it is high in cholesterol-rich fat, and best used only occasionally.

White sugar is receiving increasing condemnation as a source of empty calories and as a suspected cause of many ailments with which the sweet-toothed Western world now suffers. Substitute raw cane sugar or honey. Meat and fish are also excluded. They can be an expensive source of protein, and not at all essential for a healthy diet.

Convenience foods rarely appear, but are obviously helpful when you are trying to prepare interesting packed lunches in a short space of time. The secret is to use them sparingly, and only when absolutely necessary, but not to dismiss them entirely. If you have a choice between frozen and tinned foods (vegetables, for example), use the former.

Besides noticing the absence of certain foods in this book, you will also find some unusual additions. Miso, for example, is a spicy *purée* made from soya beans that have been naturally fermented and is delicious in soups and sandwiches. Similarly, soy sauce will add a lot of goodness along with its distinctive salty flavour. (Another soya bean product you might like to try is a milk powder that you add to water — it is creamy-tasting, versatile, and much lower in fat than milk.)

As an alternative to chocolate, carob powder is excellent. Low in fats and starch and yet rich in natural sugars, vitamins and minerals, carob powder does not have the disastrous effect that chocolate does on your complexion, digestion — or your hips!

A large number of recipes call for oil, and the best kind to use — again — is one that is high in polyunsaturates, and therefore less likely to clog your arteries. Try vegetable oils such as sunflower, safflower or corn.

Add to these the many familiar foods you know to be high in nutritional value — all kinds of cheese, plain yogurt, cream (in small amounts only), nuts, beans, cereals, eggs (preferably free-range), lots of fruit, salad and vegetables. A packed lunch based on such foods will be a feast!

Working with Your Body

And finally, to complete your day, reverse the trend and instead of having a heavy meal, make your dinner more of a snack. You do not need energy foods because you will probably be going to bed shortly. You do not want your digestive system to be over-loaded because you're hoping for a good night's sleep! Get into the habit of providing food for your body to use when it intends to use it — during the day. And when you are resting, let your whole system have a break, too. Working with your body this way is not cranky, it is simply being kind to yourself. And what better way to make yourself feel good?

NEW WAYS WITH SANDWICHES

Think of packed lunches, and the first things that come to mind are sandwiches. They are quick to make, easy to carry, and convenient to eat. Unfortunately, they usually contain little of food value, but lots of calories, which is why they've come to be considered fattening.

Put together thoughtfully, however, sandwiches can be a complete and satisfying meal in themselves. Use wholewheat bread and you are off to a healthy start. Besides being a good source of protein, and a variety of other nutrients, wholewheat bread is more satisfying than the refined, white kind, yet has roughly the same calorie count. So you will find you can eat less without going hungry. Although wholewheat bread is now available almost everywhere, a home-made loaf, hot and fragrant from the oven, is well worth the effort, at least once in a while.

Adventurous Fillings

To prevent your sandwiches from becoming boring, be adventurous about the fillings you choose. You can use a variety of ingredients, sweet and savoury, raw and cooked, and even the most outrageous combinations often taste superb when combined with the more bland taste of bread. Spreads, too, can make an interesting change. Although they may take a little longer to prepare in the first place, you can save time by making up enough for a few day's lunches, then simply vary the ingredients with which you combine them.

Obviously it is best if you can prepare your lunch in the morning, but if that just is not possible, sandwiches can be made at night, wrapped in clingfoil, and put in the refrigerator. They will still retain most of their goodness and flavour.

Breads

WHOLEWHEAT BREAD

Imperial (Metric)	American
1 oz (25g) dried yeast	2½ tablespoonsful dried yeast
1 teaspoonful honey or raw cane sugar	1 teaspoonful honey or raw cane sugar
1½ pints (¾ litre) warm water	3¾ cupsful warm water
3 lb (1½ kilos) wholemeal flour	12 cupsful wholemeal flour
1 teaspoonful sea salt	1 teaspoonful sea salt

1. Mix the salt and flour in a warmed bowl.

2. Dissolve the yeast and honey in a third of the water, cover, and leave in a draught-free spot until the mixture is frothy.

3. Make a well in the flour, add the salt, pour in the yeast plus the rest of the water and, using your hands, mix well.

4. Turn the dough on to a floured board and continue kneading until it is elastic. Leave covered in a warm place until the dough has doubled in size.

5. Knead again for a few minutes, divide the dough into two, shape into two loaves and dust with flour.

6. Place in two loaf tins, cover, and leave to rise again. Cook at 425°F/220°C (Gas Mark 7) for 10 minutes, then reduce the heat to 400°F/200°C (Gas Mark 6) for 35 minutes.

Note: Cooked bread sounds hollow when it is tapped.

WHOLEWHEAT BAPS

Use half the ingredients given above, and follow the directions up to
the first rising. When the dough has risen, re-knead it and divide it
into 12, then shape the pieces into baps. Dust them with wholemeal
flour and leave them covered on a greased baking sheet until risen.
Bake for 10-20 minutes at 425°F/220°C (Gas Mark 7) and leave to
cool with a cloth over them so that the centres are soft.

WHEATGERM BREAD

Imperial (Metric)	American
2½ lb (1¼ kilos) wholemeal flour	10 cupsful wholemeal flour
½ lb (¼ kilo) wheatgerm	2 cupsful wheatgerm
1 oz (25g) dried yeast	2½ tablespoonsful dried yeast
1 teaspoonful honey or raw cane sugar	1 teaspoonful honey or raw cane sugar
1½ pints (¾ litre) warm water	3¾ cupsful warm water

1. Combine the flour and wheatgerm, then follow the instructions
    as for Wholewheat Bread.

2. Cook for 40-45 minutes at 375°F/190°C (Gas Mark 5).

Note: This is a highly nutritious bread, rather sweeter than usual,
and very tasty in sandwiches. However, its high protein content
makes it especially suitable as an accompaniment, lightly buttered,
to salad.

CARAWAY CHEESE BREAD
Illustrated in colour

Imperial (Metric)	American
½ lb (¼ kilo) wholemeal flour	2 cupsful wholemeal flour
3 tablespoonsful baking powder	3½ tablespoonsful baking powder
Pinch of sea salt	Pinch of sea salt
6 oz (150g) polyunsaturated margarine	¾ cupful polyunsaturated margarine
1 large egg	1 large egg
6 oz (150g) Cheddar cheese, grated	1½ cupsful grated Cheddar cheese
1 oz (25g) caraway seeds	3½ tablespoonsful caraway seeds
¼ pint (150ml) milk	⅔ cupful milk

1. Sift together the flour, baking powder and salt.

2. Beat together the softened margarine, egg and cheese.

3. Stir in the seeds, then add the dry ingredients and mix thoroughly, stirring in the milk a drop at a time until the dough is firm but not too dry.

4. Grease a medium-sized tin and spoon the mixture into it evenly.

5. Bake at 350°F/180°C (Gas Mark 4) for 40-50 minutes, or until a knife comes out clean.

OATCAKES

Illustrated in colour

Imperial (Metric)	**American**
½ lb (¼ kilo) medium oatmeal	2 cupsful medium oatmeal
2-3 tablespoonsful vegetable oil	2½-3½ tablespoonsful vegetable oil
Pinch of sea salt	Pinch of sea salt

1. Place the oatmeal in a bowl and mix in the oil (the best way is with your fingers).

2. Gradually add water and the salt, stirring well to form a dough that is soft but can hold its shape.

3. Roll it out on a lightly floured board — as thick or thin as you like it and cut into rounds. (The thinner they are, the crisper they will be.)

4. Oatcakes can be baked at 300°F/150°C (Gas Mark 2) for about 20-30 minutes, or until crisp and golden (the exact time will depend on the thickness of the cakes). Alternatively you can cook your oatcakes in a hot, dry pan or a griddle, making them something like the traditional Scottish griddle cakes!

Note: This is a very basic recipe — quick and inexpensive to make, but not very interesting. You can, of course, liven up your oatcakes by serving them with a variety of different savoury (or sweet) toppings. You can also add things to them before you cook them: seeds, fried onion, currants, raisins or honey.

RAISIN BREAD

Imperial (Metric)	American
½ lb (¼ kilo) plain wholemeal flour	2 cupsful plain wholemeal flour
1 heaped teaspoonful baking powder	1 heaped teaspoonful baking powder
Pinch of sea salt	Pinch of sea salt
3 oz (75g) oatmeal	¾ cupful oatmeal
4 oz (100g) raisins	⅔ cupful raisins
2 oz (50g) polyunsaturated margarine or butter	¼ cupful polyunsaturated margarine or butter
2 oz (50g) raw cane sugar	¼ cupful raw cane sugar
1 egg, beaten	1 egg, beaten
Approx. ½ pint (¼ litre) soured milk or yogurt	Approx. 1⅓ cupsful soured milk or yogurt

1. In a large bowl, sieve together the flour, baking powder and salt.

2. Stir in the oatmeal, then the raisins.

3. In a separate bowl, cream the margarine with the sugar, and add the egg.

4. Combine all the ingredients thoroughly with enough milk or yogurt to make a fairly soft dough.

5. Knead this for a few minutes until smooth and elastic.

6. Grease and flour a loaf tin and remove the surplus flour, then fill with the mixture, smoothing the top. Bake at 350°F/180°C (Gas Mark 4) for 40-50 minutes, or until firm to touch.

Note: This bread is best eaten when fresh — better still if still warm from the oven, and spread with a creamy cheese.

'SODA' BREAD

Imperial (Metric)	American
1 oz (25g) polyunsaturated margarine	2½ tablespoonsful polyunsaturated margarine
½ lb (¼ kilo) self-raising wholemeal flour	2 cupsful self-raising wholemeal flour
Pinch of sea salt	Pinch of sea salt
¼ pint (150ml) milk	⅔ cupful milk

1. Rub the margarine into the flour with your finger-tips and stir in the salt.

2. Gradually add the milk, mixing it in well, then knead the dough briefly before forming it into the traditional round.

3. Use a knife to make a cross on top, brush with milk and put on to a baking tray.

4. Bake at 425°F/220°C (Gas Mark 7) for 10 minutes, then reduce the oven to 400°F/200°C (Gas Mark 6) for about 15 minutes more, or until the loaf is firm to touch. (This is best eaten when fresh.)

Note: For anyone who does not like the taste of soda (or has simply run out of it) this bread is an ideal substitute.

CHAPATTIS

Imperial (Metric)	American
½ lb (¼ kilo) wholemeal flour	2 cupsful wholemeal flour
1 tablespoonful vegetable oil	1 tablespoonful vegetable oil
1 oz (25g) roasted sesame seeds (optional)	2½ tablespoonsful roasted sesame seeds (optional)
Pinch of sea salt	Pinch of sea salt
¼ pint (150ml) water	⅔ cupful water

1. Mix together the flour, oil, seeds and salt.

2. Add enough water to make a soft dough and knead well until smooth.

3. Divide the dough into small balls, and roll each one out as thinly as possible on a floured board.

4. Cook them one at a time in a dry heated pan until the edges curl, then turn and cook the other side. (Chapattis can also be fried in the minimum amount of oil.)

Note: These are best eaten when fresh (even warm); they can be used as bread to scoop up *pâté* or dips, or just eaten with a bowl of soup, salad, or a savoury such as *dhall*. This quantity should make about 8 chapattis. You can either reduce the quantity of ingredients, or keep the prepared dough in the fridge ready for use when you need it.

Spreads

APPLE BUTTER

Imperial (Metric)	American
2 lb (1 kilo) cooking apples	2 lb cooking apples
Water or cider	Water or cider
6 oz (150g) raw cane sugar	1 cupful raw cane sugar
1 teaspoonful cinnamon	1 teaspoonful cinnamon
1 teaspoonful ginger	1 teaspoonful ginger
1 teaspoonful allspice	1 teaspoonful allspice

1. Wash but do not peel the apples. Core and slice them and place them in a saucepan with a little water or cider.

2. Cook very gently until the apples are soft and then mash them with a wooden spoon to make a smooth *purée*.

3. Add the sugar and spices and continue cooking until the *purée* is a rich brown colour, and thick enough to stick to a plate when it is turned upside-down.

4. Place the spread in a sterilized jar and store in a cool place.

GREEN-AND-RED SPREAD

Imperial (Metric)	American
4 oz (100g) cream cheese	½ cupful cream cheese
1 tablespoonful mayonnaise	1 tablespoonful mayonnaise
1 tablespoonful finely chopped leek or watercress	1 tablespoonful finely chopped leek or watercress
1 tablespoonful finely chopped red pepper or radish	1 tablespoonful finely chopped red pepper or radish
Seasoning to taste	Seasoning to taste

1. Mash the cream cheese with the mayonnaise, then add the vegetables and distribute them evenly.

2. Keep the spread in the refrigerator.

CHEESE AND RAISIN SPREAD

Imperial (Metric)	American
½ lb (¼ kilo) Cheddar cheese, grated	2 cupsful grated Cheddar cheese
2 oz (50g) polyunsaturated margarine	¼ cupful polyunsaturated margarine
3 tablespoonsful milk	3½ tablespoonsful milk
1 oz (25g) raisins	2½ tablespoonsful raisins
Seasoning to taste	Seasoning to taste

1. Combine the cheese with the margarine and milk to make a smooth, creamy paste.

2. Chop the raisins and stir them into the spread, adding the seasoning.

3. Keep the spread in the refrigerator.

Note: This basic spread can be varied in countless ways; omit the raisins and add instead: finely chopped celery
finely chopped onion
a sprinkling of nuts
finely chopped pineapple
finely chopped green or red pepper
finely chopped dates

DATE SPREAD

Imperial (Metric)	American
4 oz (100g) dates, chopped	½ cupful chopped dates
Squeeze of lemon or orange juice	Squeeze of lemon or orange juice
Water	Water

1. Cook the dates gently with the juice and a little water.

2. When the dates begin to go soft, mash them with a wooden spoon to make a sticky paste. Leave them to cook, then store the spread in a sealed jar in the refrigerator until needed.

EGG PÂTÉ

Imperial (Metric)	American
1 small avocado	1 small avocado
2 eggs, hard-boiled	2 eggs, hard-boiled
1 tablespoonful mayonnaise	1 tablespoonful mayonnaise
1 small apple	1 small apple
Sprig of parsley	Sprig of parsley
Pinch of garlic salt	Pinch of garlic salt
Seasoning to taste	Seasoning to taste

1. Chop the avocado and eggs into small pieces and mash them.

2. Combine the avocado and eggs with the mayonnaise.

3. Grate the apple finely, chop the parsley, and add them to the egg mixture together with the garlic and seasoning as required.

Note: This will keep for a few days in a cool place.

CREAMY CHEESY SPREAD

Imperial (Metric)	American
4 oz (100g) cottage cheese	½ cupful cottage cheese
2 oz (50g) Cheddar cheese, grated	½ cupful grated Cheddar cheese
4 tablespoonsful mayonnaise	5 tablespoonsful mayonnaise
Chopped chives	Chopped chives

1. Combine all the ingredients and keep the spread in the refrigerator until needed.

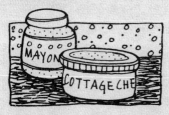

SPICED COTTAGE CHEESE

Imperial (Metric)	American
4 oz (100g) cottage cheese	½ cupful cottage cheese
2 tablespoonsful mayonnaise	2½ tablespoonsful mayonnaise
½ teaspoonful mixed spice	½ teaspoonful mixed spice
1 tablespoonful soy sauce	1 tablespoonful soy sauce
Squeeze of lemon juice	Squeeze of lemon juice

1. Mix all the ingredients very thoroughly.

2. Chill the mixture well before serving.

Note: Vary the taste by mixing some ground ginger into the spice, or by replacing it completely with ginger.

PEANUT BUTTER

Imperial (Metric)	American
4 oz (100g) roasted peanuts	¾ cupful roasted peanuts
Vegetable oil (if needed)	Vegetable oil (if needed)
Sea salt	Sea salt

1. Use a grinder to grind the nuts as finely as possible. Transfer them to a bowl and mash them well.

2. As peanuts are quite oily, the paste will probably form itself into a butter without the addition of further oil, but if it is still very crumbly, add just a few drops and combine well.

3. Add salt to taste and place the butter in a jar.

Note: You can make butters in this way using almost any kind of nut, either raw or roasted. Try walnuts, hazelnuts, cashews, sunflower or sesame seeds. The drier nuts will probably need more oil added to make them into a smooth butter.

KIDNEY BEAN PÂTÉ

Imperial (Metric)	American
4 oz (100g) cooked kidney beans	½ cupful cooked kidney beans
2 oz (50g) cheese, grated	½ cupful grated cheese
4 oz (100g) wholemeal breadcrumbs	2 cupsful wholemeal breadcrumbs
A little vegetable stock	A little vegetable stock
Soy sauce	Soy sauce
1 onion, chopped	1 onion, chopped
Herbs and seasoning to taste	Herbs and seasoning to taste

1. Mash the beans and grate the cheese.

2. Soak the breadcrumbs in a little vegetable stock, adding a few drops of soy sauce.

3. Lightly fry the onion and add it to the mashed beans with the cheese, mixing very well.

4. Squeeze most of the moisture out of the breadcrumbs and stir them into the bean mixture with the herbs and seasoning. Chill before serving.

NUT CURRY SPREAD

Imperial (Metric)	American
2 oz (50g) polyunsaturated margarine	¼ cupful polyunsaturated margarine
2 oz (50g) ground nuts	½ cupful ground nuts
1-2 teaspoonsful curry powder	1-2 teaspoonsful curry powder

1. Make a smooth paste by combining all the ingredients.

Note: This spread tastes delicious on wholemeal bread, topped with cool cucumber slices.

TESSA'S SANDWICH SPREAD

Imperial (Metric)	American
4 oz (100g) raw peanuts	¾ cupful raw peanuts
¼ cucumber	¼ cucumber
1 carrot	1 carrot
1 stick of celery	1 stick of celery
1 small onion	1 small onion
Vegetable oil	Vegetable oil
Cider vinegar	Cider vinegar
Seasoning to taste	Seasoning to taste

1. Grind the nuts to a smooth paste.

2. Chop the vegetables as finely as possible and combine them with the nuts.

3. Add enough oil and vinegar to make the mixture the consistency of a spread.

4. Season according to taste.

AVOCADO SPREAD

Imperial (Metric)	American
1 ripe avocado	1 ripe avocado
2 oz (50g) cottage cheese	¼ cupful cottage cheese
Squeeze of lemon juice	Squeeze of lemon juice
Seasoning to taste	Seasoning to taste
1 oz (25g) walnuts, chopped	¼ cupful English walnuts, chopped

1. Skin and stone the avocado, and mash the flesh.

2. Add the cottage cheese, lemon juice and seasoning, and continue mashing until you have a smooth paste.

3. Stir in the nuts, and chill the spread before serving.

CREAM CHEESE CRUNCH

Imperial (Metric)
1 stick of celery, finely chopped
2 Weetabix (or similar), crushed
4 oz (100g) cream cheese
Squeeze of lemon juice
Pinch of oregano
Seasoning to taste

American
1 stick of celery, finely chopped
2 Weetabix (or similar), crushed
½ cupful cream cheese
Squeeze of lemon juice
Pinch of oregano
Seasoning to taste

1. Combine all the ingredients to make a spread that is both crunchy and smooth.

Note: This spread will keep for a few days in the refrigerator, but the biscuits will go soft.

VEGETABLE PÂTÉ
Illustrated in colour

Imperial (Metric)
4 oz (100g) polyunsaturated
    margarine or butter
1 onion, sliced
1 courgette, finely chopped
2 oz (50g) mushrooms
2 oz (50g) peas, cooked
Herbs to taste
Pinch of garlic salt
Seasoning to taste

American
½ cupful polyunsaturated
    margarine or butter
1 onion, sliced
1 zucchini, finely chopped
1 cupful mushrooms
⅓ cupful peas, cooked
Herbs to taste
Pinch of garlic salt
Seasoning to taste

1. Heat the margarine and gently fry the onion and courgette.

2. When the vegetables are tender, add the mushrooms and cook them for a few minutes.

3. Add the cooked peas, herbs, garlic and seasoning and mash all the ingredients thoroughly (preferably in a blender).

Note: This spread will keep in the refrigerator for 4-5 days.

CHEESE BUTTER

Imperial (Metric)	American
4 oz (100g) Cheddar cheese	1 cupful grated Cheddar cheese
2 oz (50g) polyunsaturated margarine or butter	¼ cupful polyunsaturated margarine or butter
1 tablespoonful milk	1 tablespoonful milk
Celery salt and freshly ground black pepper	Celery salt and freshly ground black pepper

1. Combine all the ingredients in a basin and heat them over a saucepan of boiling water. (As the cheese and margarine melt, stir well.)

Note: Keep the spread in the refrigerator.

HONEY AND WALNUT SPREAD

Imperial (Metric)	American
3 oz (75g) walnuts, chopped	⅔ cupful English walnuts, chopped
2-3 tablespoonsful thick honey	2½-3½ tablespoonsful thick honey
2 tablespoonsful double cream (optional)	2½ tablespoonsful heavy cream (optional)

1. Use a grinder to powder the nuts, then mix them with the honey to make a thick paste.

2. This spread can be eaten as it is, but for a less sweet and creamier spread, add some cream.

Note: This spread should be kept refrigerated and used within a few days.

BROAD BEAN PÂTÉ

Imperial (Metric)	American
4 oz (100g) dried broad beans, soaked overnight	½ cupful Windsor beans, soaked overnight
½-1 clove garlic, crushed	½-1 clove garlic, crushed
Squeeze of lemon juice	Squeeze of lemon juice
1 tablespoonful aniseed (or to taste)	1 tablespoonful aniseed (or to taste)
1 tablespoonful freshly chopped mint or parsley	1 tablespoonful freshly chopped mint or parsley
1 tablespoonful vegetable oil	1 tablespoonful vegetable oil
Mayonnaise (optional)	Mayonnaise (optional)
Seasoning to taste	Seasoning to taste

1. Cook the broad beans until soft (or use left-over beans). When cool, either mash or blend them to make a paste.

2. Add the garlic, lemon juice, aniseed, mint or parsley.

3. Stir in the oil to thicken the *pâté*. (If you like a lighter texture, add some mayonnaise.)

4. Season to taste and chill until needed.

GHERKIN SPREAD

Imperial (Metric)	American
4 oz (100g) polyunsaturated margarine or butter	½ cupful polyunsaturated margarine or butter
2 oz (50g) cheese, grated	½ cupful grated cheese
3 pickled gherkins	3 pickled gherkins
A few capers	A few capers
Seasoning to taste	Seasoning to taste

1. Mash together the margarine and cheese.

2. Add the very finely chopped gherkins and capers and season to taste.

Note: Although this spread should be kept in the cool if not being used immediately, the flavour is better if it has been left at room temperature for a while just before it is eaten.

SUGGESTED FILLINGS

Cream cheese, hazelnut butter, celery pieces.
Cheddar cheese, tomato, bean sprouts.
Mashed banana, grated carrot, sprinkling of coconut.
Egg mayonnaise, chicory, tomato.
Date spread, walnuts, cream cheese.
Cheese butter, thinly sliced pear.
Miso, lettuce, tahini, squeeze of lemon juice.
Cottage cheese mixed with scrambled eggs and chives.
Cream cheese and lightly crushed strawberries.
Egg *pâté* with finely sliced courgette.
Miso, mustard and cress, roasted cashew nuts.
Edam cheese, apple slices, a little curry powder.
Bean sprouts and tahini.
Cottage cheese, herbs, chopped spring onion.
Peanut butter and lettuce, celery, cucumber.

Mashed avocado pear, a sprinkling of sunflower seeds.
Yeast extract, cucumber slices, cress.
Tahini, watercress, cheese, chopped olives.
Cashew butter and sliced peach.
Thinly sliced nut loaf, Chinese leaves.
Cheese, cole-slaw, caraway seeds.
Chestnut *purée*, cream cheese, cucumber slices.
Curd cheese, radishes, endive leaves.
Banana, honey, flaked almonds.
Dhall with tomato and cucumber slices.
Cheddar cheese, chutney, lettuce.
Date spread, chopped brazils, celery pieces.
Chopped pepper, tomato and watercress in soured cream dressing.
Peanut butter, curry powder and raisins.
Tahini and freshly sliced apple.
Banana, lemon juice, chopped dates and nuts.
Grated carrots, raisins, mayonnaise to bind.
Cream cheese, peanut butter, chopped olives.
Ricotta cheese and dates.
Scrambled egg, curry powder and a few peas.
Thin slices of tofu, bean sprouts, a little yeast extract.
Tinned nut meat with watercress and tomatoes.
Mozzarella cheese, chicory, watercress.
Blue cheese mashed with a little curd cheese, walnuts.
Cashew butter, sliced red pepper, Chinese leaves.
Apple butter with raisins.
Butter with lemon juice, chives and cucumber slices.
Raw sugar apricot jam, banana slices, walnuts.
Dutch cheese, mushroom slices, watercress.
Cold omelette, sliced, with celery pieces.
Chocolate spread with chopped, roasted hazelnuts.
Tofu mashed with a little miso, shreds of raw spinach.
Cooked lentils mashed with onion, curry powder (or left-over lentil
    curry).

SUNSHINE SALADS

Amongst people who 'enjoy their food', salads have a bad reputation. They are the mainstay of weight watchers, so they are automatically associated with hunger, self-denial, even misery. Salads are good for you — and what could be more guaranteed to make them unpopular? Like spinach and bran, salads are a food everyone knows they ought to eat, but no one expects to actually enjoy.

Maybe that is why the British eating tradition relegates salads to the position of an extra. You have your main dish, the centre-piece of your meal, and with it you have a side salad, to pick at if you have any room left (which, of course, is rarely the case).

Use Your Imagination
The ingredients that go into our salads are traditional, too. Despite the ever-increasing variety of vegetables now available (most of which taste super raw as well as cooked), we serve up the same soggy lettuce, over-cooked beetroot, and tinned potatoes. Yet by being adventurous enough to throw any fresh young vegetables in with the more usual ingredients, we could have a feast of distinctive flavour, contrasting textures, and colours to capture any salad hater's interest! Before you know it, salads will be a worth-while dish in their own right.

It is a healthy idea to have a big raw salad every day. As it needs no cooking, is easy to carry, and can be as varied as you choose to make it, salad is a great idea for your packed lunch.

Buy a large polythene container, or re-use the cartons in which so many foods are sold these days (e.g., margarine, cottage cheese). Choose your favourite ingredients, preferably avoiding anything too juicy or too soft. Add some cheese, nuts, cooked beans, an egg, wholemeal bread or crispbread. In winter, take a small flask of soup to get your lunch off to a hot start. Be adventurous about salad dressings, too. Many dips and sandwich spreads can be made more liquid with additional water, milk or oil — try them and see what tasty treats you can invent!

One final point. Salads are only nutritious and tasty when they are *fresh*. Learn to choose ingredients that are at their peak. Keep them for as short a time as possible and in a cool temperature. To ensure that your lunch time salad retains most of its goodness, prepare it in the morning — keep the ingredients simple, and you won't need to get up much earlier than usual.

Sprouting

Possibly the only time you have eaten bean sprouts was as part of a Chinese meal. If so, forget them, and try the very different taste of freshly grown raw sprouts. Sprouted beans and seeds are highly nutritive, low in calories, easy and inexpensive to grow at home — and they are the ideal way to make more of your salads.

Buy your seeds from a health food shop, or anywhere that guarantees them to be organically grown and untouched by chemicals. Only live seeds will sprout. Mung beans are the traditional choice, but you can produce a great variety of sprouts from such things as aduki and soya beans, fenugreek, sunflower, sesame and alfalfa seeds, and from grains like whole wheat and barley. Next you need a container with natural drainage. Any large, wide-necked jar can be used if you secure a piece of cheesecloth or fine mesh over the top.

Wash a small amount of the seeds you have chosen, discard any stones, and place the seeds in the jar. They will increase their bulk six to eight times, so do allow them plenty of room. Cover them with tepid water and leave in a warm dark place to soak overnight. In the morning they should be rinsed and drained two or three times, then returned to the dark. Continue this rinsing process, morning and night, until the seeds have sprouted to anything from a half to two-and-a-half inches in length. Then eat them as salad ingredients, in sandwiches, or very lightly boiled. When grown, they can be kept in the refrigerator a few days.

For successful sprouting, take care to choose a spot that is not too hot or too cold. The main problem occurs when seeds are either dried out or flooded, so rinse them carefully, making sure you leave them moist, but not soaking in water. Handle them gently, too, as sprouts are fragile.

Dressings

MAYONNAISE

Imperial (Metric)
1 large egg, whisked
2 tablespoonsful cider vinegar
   or lemon juice
1 teaspoonful honey
Seasoning to taste
½ pint (¼ litre) vegetable oil

American
1 large egg, whisked
2½ tablespoonsful cider vinegar
   or lemon juice
1 teaspoonful honey
Seasoning to taste
1⅓ cupsful vegetable oil

1. Add the vinegar or lemon juice, honey and seasoning to the egg and blend thoroughly.

2. Add the oil gradually, beating all the time, until the mixture is thick and smooth. (If using a blender, combine all the ingredients except the oil, then remove the central cap and pour the oil in slowly whilst keeping the blender on a high speed.)

Note: This makes approximately ¾ pint (400ml) of mayonnaise, which will keep for a week or so in a cool place (not the refrigerator).

1. Oatcakes (page 15) and Vegetable Pâté (page 25) make a quick and easy working lunch, rounded off with a fruity natural yogurt.

2. Meal-in-a-Soup (page 54) and Caraway Cheese Bread (page 14) will keep out the cold on a winter schoolday.

MAYONNAISE WITH CHIVES

Imperial (Metric)
1 tablespoonful chopped chives
3 tablespoonsful soured cream
¼ pint (150ml) mayonnaise

American
1 tablespoonful chopped chives
3½ tablespoonsful soured cream
⅔ cupful mayonnaise

1. Combine all the ingredients well. (You can adjust the amount of chives to suit your taste, or vary the flavour by using finely chopped parsley or onion instead.)

NUT MAYONNAISE

Imperial (Metric)
2 oz (50g) hazelnuts
¼ pint (150ml) mayonnaise
Squeeze of lemon juice

American
⅓ cupful hazelnuts
⅔ cupful mayonnaise
Squeeze of lemon juice

1. Grind the nuts to a fine powder, and add them to the mayonnaise with the lemon juice.

LOW-CALORIE DRESSING

Imperial (Metric)
1 cupful cottage cheese
¼ pint (150ml) natural yogurt
1 tablespoonful honey
1 teaspoonful lemon juice
Herbs or 1 oz (25g) nuts, chopped

American
1¼ cupsful cottage cheese
⅔ cupful natural yogurt
1 tablespoonful honey
1 teaspoonful lemon juice
Herbs or ¼ cupful chopped nuts

1. Sieve the cottage cheese (or mash it to a smooth consistency).

2. Blend all the ingredients together well; keep this dressing in the refrigerator and use it as required.

TAHINI DRESSING

Imperial (Metric)	American
2 sticks of celery	2 sticks of celery
4 oz (100g) tahini (sesame paste)	½ cupful tahini
Squeeze of lemon juice	Squeeze of lemon juice
Seasoning to taste	Seasoning to taste
A little water	A little water

1. Chop the celery as finely as possible.

2. Mix the celery with the lemon juice and seasoning.

3. Add water to make the dressing the desired consistency.

CHICK PEA DIP

Imperial (Metric)	American
4 oz (100g) chick peas, cooked	½ cupful garbanzo beans, cooked
2 tablespoonsful tahini	2½ tablespoonsful tahini
1 tablespoonful vegetable oil	1 tablespoonful vegetable oil
Squeeze of lemon juice	Squeeze of lemon juice
1 clove of garlic, crushed (or pinch of garlic powder)	1 clove of garlic, crushed (or pinch of garlic powder)
Seasoning to taste	Seasoning to taste

1. Mash the chick peas to a paste, preferably in a blender.

2. Combine all the ingredients and mix them well.

Note: This may be eaten with celery and carrot sticks as a dip, or, with sufficient water added as a dressing. (Keep in the refrigerator.)

SOURED CREAM DRESSING

Imperial (Metric)
1 small bunch of chives or
    watercress, finely chopped
1 small carton soured cream
Squeeze of lemon juice
Milk to mix
Seasoning to taste

American
1 small bunch of chives or
    watercress, finely chopped
1 small carton soured cream
Squeeze of lemon juice
Milk to mix
Seasoning to taste

1. Combine all the ingredients with enough milk to make a thin cream, and keep in the refrigerator until needed.

VINAIGRETTE DRESSING

Imperial (Metric)
2 tablespoonsful cider vinegar or
    lemon juice
4 tablespoonsful vegetable oil
Chopped parsley
Seasoning to taste

American
2½ tablespoonsful cider vinegar or
    lemon juice
5 tablespoonsful vegetable oil
Chopped parsley
Seasoning to taste

1. Combine the vinegar or lemon juice and oil thoroughly — they will appear to thicken a little — then add the remaining ingredients.

Note: You can also combine all the ingredients in a screw-top jar and shake them vigorously until blended. This will keep for a week or two in the cool.

COCONUT DRESSING

Imperial (Metric)	American
Milk to mix	Milk to mix
2 oz (50g) cream cheese	¼ cupful cream cheese
1 tablespoonful honey	1 tablespoonful honey
2 oz (50g) desiccated coconut	⅔ cupful desiccated coconut

1. Add enough milk to the softened cream cheese to make it into a pouring consistency.

2. Stir in the honey until dissolved, then add the coconut.

GREEN GODDESS DRESSING

Imperial (Metric)	American
1 small carton cottage cheese	1 small carton cottage cheese
1 small bunch of chives	1 small bunch of chives
1 sprig of parsley (or dried equivalent)	1 sprig of parsley (or dried equivalent)
Few leaves of tarragon (or dried equivalent)	Few leaves of tarragon (or dried equivalent)
1 teaspoonful cider vinegar	1 teaspoonful cider vinegar
3 tablespoonsful mayonnaise	3½ tablespoonsful mayonnaise

1. Sieve the cottage cheese until smooth (or use a blender).

2. Add the finely chopped greens, vinegar and mayonnaise, and blend all the ingredients very thoroughly.

GINGER SALAD DRESSING

Imperial (Metric)	American
2 tablespoonsful soy sauce	2½ tablespoonsful soy sauce
2 tablespoonsful cider vinegar	2½ tablespoonsful cider vinegar
1 teaspoonful clear honey	1 teaspoonful clear honey
2 tablespoonsful vegetable oil	2½ tablespoonsful vegetable oil
Good pinch of ground ginger to taste	Good pinch of ground ginger to taste

1. Put all the ingredients together in a jar and shake them well.

2. Taste the dressing and adjust the seasoning — you may also like to add a little more cider vinegar or honey.

WALNUT SALAD DRESSING

Imperial (Metric)	American
3 oz (75g) walnuts	⅔ cupful walnuts
½-1 clove of garlic, crushed	½-1 clove of garlic, crushed
2 oz (50g) wholemeal breadcrumbs	1 cupful wholemeal breadcrumbs
Squeeze of lemon juice	Squeeze of lemon juice
Vegetable stock or milk as necessary	Vegetable stock or milk as necessary
Seasoning to taste	Seasoning to taste

1. Crush the walnuts to a powder, or grind them, and mix them well with the garlic, breadcrumbs and lemon juice.

2. Add the liquid gradually until the dressing is like a thin cream.

3. Season to taste, adding a little paprika or cayenne pepper if liked.

Note: This is an unusual high-protein dressing that turns a simple green salad into a balanced dish.

TOFU DRESSING

Imperial (Metric)
5 oz (125g) tofu
2 tablespoonsful vegetable oil
1-2 tablespoonsful cider vinegar
Soy sauce (optional)
Seasoning to taste

American
¾ cupful tofu
2½ tablespoonsful vegetable oil
1-2½ tablespoonsful cider vinegar
Soy sauce (optional)
Seasoning to taste

1. Mash the drained tofu to make a cream, then mix it well with the other ingredients, tasting as you do so, and adjusting the flavour accordingly. (You can also use a blender for this job.)

Note: This is a basic recipe and can be adapted in countless ways. Add, for example, fresh or dried herbs, curry powder, mustard, minced onion and/or garlic, tahini, peanut butter, tomato *purée*, parsley, chopped olives, chopped hard-boiled egg, crushed pineapple, honey, etc. This is another protein-packed dressing.

GUACAMOLE DRESSING WITH YOGURT

Imperial (Metric)
1 medium-ripe avocado
1 tablespoonful lemon juice
½ small onion, finely chopped
1 large tomato, mashed
½ clove of garlic, minced
Approx. ¼ pint (150ml) natural
  yogurt
Seasoning to taste

American
1 medium-ripe avocado
1 tablespoonful lemon juice
½ small onion, finely chopped
1 large tomato, mashed
½ clove of garlic, minced
Approx. ⅔ cupful natural
  yogurt
Seasoning to taste

1. Peel, chop and then mash the avocado, adding lemon juice straight away to stop it browning.

2. Add the onion and tomato to the avocado, mixing well.

3. Stir in the garlic and enough yogurt to give the dressing the consistency you prefer.

4. Season to taste and chill the dressing until needed.

HOT CHILLI DRESSING

Imperial (Metric)
1-2 spring onions
¼ pint (150ml) mayonnaise
5 tablespoonsful soured or double
  cream
Squeeze of lemon juice
Chilli sauce to taste
Cayenne pepper to taste

American
1-2 scallions
⅔ cupful mayonnaise
6 tablespoonsful soured or heavy
  cream
Squeeze of lemon juice
Chilli sauce to taste
Cayenne pepper to taste

1. Chop the onions and mix them with the other ingredients, adjusting the flavour to make it as mild or as hot as you like.

Note: This is not a very good dressing for delicately flavoured green salads, but tastes great with such things as cooked cold potatoes or beans (kidney in particular). It is best chilled until needed.

SALAD SUGGESTIONS

Drain some tinned sweet corn. Finely chop some green or red pepper (or use a small piece of each colour). Mix the sweet corn, pepper, and a handful of raisins together. Add a few walnuts for protein.

Wash some young courgettes. Slice them into ¼-inch pieces. Chop one or two firm tomatoes into quarters. Combine the vegetables with Green Goddess Dressing.

Chop a handful of clean button mushrooms into quarters; finely chop one or two spring onions. To some soured cream add seasoning and a pinch of paprika, then combine this with the vegetables.

Mix together some dark, freshly washed watercress, a small orange chopped into pieces and a few leaves of chicory. Moisten with Vinaigrette Dressing. Good with cold flan.

Chop a stick of celery, some cucumber, and an apple into small pieces. Mix them well with some lightly roasted cashew nuts, and one or two chopped prunes. Toss in yogurt.

Tear a crisp lettuce into large pieces. Combine with chunks of avocado, a few chopped walnuts, and a quartered hard-boiled egg.

Finely slice some red and green cabbage and a little raw onion. Mix well. Add a few grapes, a sprinkling of caraway seeds and Vinaigrette Dressing.

Break a small cauliflower into florets; wash and dry them. Finely grate a piece of green pepper. Mash a few ounces of grated cheese with a little milk to make into a smooth paste, season, and pour this over vegetables. Mix well.

To a portion of cold brown rice (left over from a previous meal) add chopped pear, some roasted peanuts, and a good helping of bean sprouts. Toss in Vinaigrette Dressing.

Young, tender broad beans taste delicious raw. Mix them with some chopped parsley, add a creamy dressing, and serve on a base of fresh, crisp lettuce.

Combine some avocado chunks with finely sliced red pepper and grapefruit sections. Add shredded lettuce, and a mayonnaise dressing.

Grate a couple of carrots, add some chopped banana and a few sultanas. Mix these well in a good portion of Coconut Dressing.

Combine some bean sprouts with a few endive leaves, torn into large pieces. Mix in some chopped hazelnuts and a sliced peach, or two apricots. Add a squeeze of lemon juice to keep the fruit from going brown.

To shredded lettuce add some chopped pineapple (preferably fresh) and a large piece of cucumber, also chopped. Mix with Coconut or Soured Cream Dressing.

Left-over beans can be made into a salad by adding some finely-chopped celery or onion, sliced tomato, and the dressing of your choice. Use kidney, aduki, butter beans, chick peas, black-eyed peas — whatever you have handy, alone or in a combination.

Chinese leaves are especially crisp and sweet. Shred them, then combine them with some radishes, mustard and cress, and a good portion of Chick Pea Dip.

Shred some chicory leaves, add some finely grated raw brussels sprouts, quartered tomatoes, and a few olives. Eat this with Tahini Dressing.

Mix some orange segments with chopped cucumber and a handful of almonds. Low-calorie Dressing is nice with these ingredients.

Celery pieces with a few dates, chopped banana, and a little finely chopped fennel are very refreshing. Try them with Soured Cream Dressing.

Peel a raw beetroot and grate it finely. Add some sliced apple, some raisins and a few sprigs of watercress. Moisten with Vinaigrette Dressing.

Take some fresh spinach leaves, wash and dry them thoroughly, discarding the stems. Chop a portion of cucumber, a stick of celery, a few olives. Combine all the ingredients with the dressing of your choice.

To a small carton of cottage cheese, add a good portion of chopped green vegetables (e.g. cucumber, celery, chicory, pepper). Mix in some fruit (gooseberries, raspberries, blackberries and grapes all taste good). Stir in a teaspoonful of honey and add a sprinkling of freshly ground black pepper.

Choose some young leeks: strip off the outer leaves and wash the white part thoroughly. Chop them finely and mix them with grated carrot, apple, and sunflower seeds. Add Vinaigrette Dressing.

Use cooked vegetables for a change. A nice combination is cooked peas, carrots, and finely chopped asparagus with a mayonnaise dressing. Serve it on a crisp lettuce base and maybe sprinkle over some nuts or sunflower seeds.

The basic cole-slaw made with finely grated cabbage and carrots can be adapted by adding a variety of ingredients. Try dried fruits such as prunes or apricots finely chopped; apple slices; nuts and raisins; tiny cubes of blue cheese and grapes; bean sprouts with Tofu Dressing; tomato, chopped pepper and onion with parsley; grape-fruit and avocado segments with a sprinkling of sesame seeds; cauliflower florets with Tahini Dressing; beetroot cubes and Soured Cream dressing; freshly sliced peach, walnuts; celery slices, orange segments and roasted cashews; or simply sprinkle some caraway seeds over the top and serve with a spoonful of soured cream or yogurt.

Chopped spring onion, carrot, celery and cucumber with a sprinkling of bean sprouts and tiny cubes of tofu — this is nice with Ginger Salad Dressing.

Baby beetroots served with a garlic butter, sprinkled with fresh parsley. Make the garlic butter by melting 2 oz (50g) of butter and mixing in ½-1 clove of crushed garlic; the finer the garlic is crushed, the smoother the butter will be. Pour this over the beetroots whilst still warm.

Raw broccoli florets with a little finely chopped onion, some chives, and sprinkling of soya 'bacon' bits. A creamy dressing goes well with this combination.

Lettuce, sliced raw mushrooms, red pepper and fennel with black olives. Walnut Salad Dressing is exotic with this salad.

THE LIQUID LUNCH

An increasingly widespread interpretation of the liquid lunch is a couple of pints of beer, or glasses of wine, accompanied, perhaps, by a packet of crisps or a pork pie. Refreshing as it may be at the time, such lunches should be the occasional treat rather than the daily routine.

Alcohol gives you calories, and not much else. It sharpens your appetite (which means cake with your afternoon tea — more empty calories!) and it dulls your brain, making the afternoon's work more difficult, less satisfying.

Many housewives have a liquid lunch of a different kind. Too busy to stop what they are doing, or too lazy to prepare themselves some real food, they will have a cup of coffee with a biscuit. The caffeine, and sugar if they take it, will make them feel able to last out until dinner time — and if they get peckish, they can always have another coffee!

There are, of course, people whose metabolisms work in such a way that, not only do they rarely fancy a midday meal, but, if they did eat, they would probably be unable to digest and use the food properly. For them, here are some liquid lunches with a difference.

Juices

Raw juices have long been associated with building health. Because a large amount of fruit or vegetables is condensed into a small amount of juice, you get a feast of vitamins and minerals in one glassful. What is more, the goodness is more quickly and easily assimilated into your system than when your body has to extract it from the solid matter first. That is why such juices are ideal for the sick, or anyone with digestive problems. Fasting on fresh juices for one or two days rests and cleanses the system too — try it instead of a tonic next time you are feeling low. (But no longer than two days without medical supervision, please.)

Add protein-rich egg, milk, or soya milk to such drinks and you have a complete meal in a glass. Try the recipes given here, then experiment with your own. The variations are limitless! Although ideal for lunching at home, these drinks are not suitable for taking to work as they should be prepared just before they are drunk to obtain maximum goodness.

Soups

Soups, on the other hand, will travel well. Buy one of the very small Thermos flasks now available, and you can have a hot, satisfying liquid lunch wherever you are.

Recipes given here are for two servings, on the assumption that you wish to save time in the kitchen. You can always keep the extra portion in the refrigerator for a day or two (or, of course, you could share it).

Each soup has been chosen because it provides protein as well as satisfaction, so it can be consumed as part of your lunch, or as the complete meal. You can increase the protein further by adding skimmed milk powder or cream, *croûtons* made from wholemeal bread, grated cheese or hard-boiled egg.

Juices and Drinks

PROTEIN VEGETABLE DRINK

Imperial (Metric)	American
1 egg, beaten	1 egg, beaten
¼ pint (150ml) vegetable juice, tinned or freshly made	⅔ cupful vegetable juice, tinned or freshly made
Soy sauce	Soy sauce

1. Add the egg to the vegetable juice and pour the mixture into a blender.

2. Whisk well, add a few drops of soy sauce and drink at once.

Note: This is a protein-packed drink which will keep you going all afternoon.

SLIMMER'S COCKTAIL

Imperial (Metric)	American
¼ pint (150ml) tomato juice, tinned or freshly made	⅔ cupful tomato juice, tinned or freshly made
1 oz (25g) cottage cheese	2½ tablespoonsful cottage cheese
1 tablespoonful bran (optional)	1 tablespoonful bran (optional)
Soy sauce	Soy sauce

1. Combine all the ingredients, place them in a blender and whisk well.

2. Chill before drinking.

Note: Carrot or other vegetable juice can be substituted for the tomato to make a tasty change.

VITAMIN DRINK

Imperial (Metric)	American
1 carrot, finely chopped	1 carrot, finely chopped
1 stick of celery, finely chopped	1 stick of celery, finely chopped
Parsley, finely chopped	Parsley, finely chopped

1. Place all the ingredients in a liquidizer. Drink this chilled.

Note: For a spicier tasting drink, add a little paprika. For a sweeter drink, add some raisins before liquidizing.

BANANA MILK

Imperial (Metric)	American
1 ripe banana	1 ripe banana
Squeeze of lemon juice	Squeeze of lemon juice
½ pint (¼ litre) milk (whole, skimmed or soya)	1⅓ cupful milk (whole, skimmed or soya)
1 tablespoonful granola or other cereal	1 tablespoonful granola or other cereal

1. Mash the banana to a smooth *purée* and add the lemon juice to stop it turning brown.

2. Whisk the banana into the milk, preferably with a blender.

3. Stir in the cereal to add crunchiness, and drink at once.

CARROT MILK SHAKE

Imperial (Metric)
¼ pint (150ml) carrot juice, tinned
  or freshly made
5 tablespoonsful milk (whole,
  skimmed or soya)
1 teaspoonful honey

American
⅔ cupful carrot juice, tinned or
  freshly made
6 tablespoonsful milk (whole,
  skimmed or soya)
1 teaspoonful honey

1. Combine all the ingredients, place them in a blender and whisk thoroughly.

Note: If using fresh carrots, the younger ones will make a sweeter drink.

PROTEIN LEMON DRINK

Imperial (Metric)
1 egg, beaten
Juice of 1 lemon
1-2 teaspoonsful honey

American
1 egg, beaten
Juice of 1 lemon
1-2 teaspoonsful honey

1. Combine all the ingredients in a blender and whisk until pale and frothy. Drink this at once.

Note: You can vary this high-protein drink by using other fruit juices instead of lemon. Try orange, pineapple, blackcurrant or grapefruit.

APPLE AND CASHEW CREAM

Imperial (Metric)	**American**
2 oz (50g) cashew nuts	¹/₂ cupful cashew nuts
Water	Water
2 tablespoonsful apple juice	2¹/₂ tablespoonsful apple juice

1. Grind the nuts to a fine powder — a coffee grinder does the job quickly and efficiently.

2. Add enough water to make the mixture into the consistency of single cream, then stir in the apple juice. (For a special treat, add a teaspoonful of jam — this tastes delicious, but it does bump up the calorie count!)

Note: Almost any combination of ground nuts and fruit juice makes a tasty, energizing drink. Experiment with your favourites.

FLORIDA MILK

Imperial (Metric)	**American**
1-2 teaspoonsful honey	1-2 teaspoonsful honey
¹/₂ pint (¹/₄ litre) milk (whole, skimmed or soya)	1¹/₃ cupful milk (whole, skimmed or soya)
Juice of ¹/₂ lemon	Juice of ¹/₂ lemon
Juice of ¹/₂ orange	Juice of ¹/₂ orange
Chopped nuts (optional)	Chopped nuts (optional)

1. Dissolve the honey in the milk by stirring well, then gradually add the fruit juices.

2. Whisk by hand, and top with a sprinkling of nuts if liked.

HOT 'CHOCOLATE'

Imperial (Metric)	American
½ pint (¼ litre) milk (whole, skimmed or soya)	1⅓ cupsful milk (whole, skimmed or soya)
1 tablespoonful carob powder	1 tablespoonful carob powder
½ tablespoonful raw cane sugar	½ tablespoonful raw cane sugar

1. Make a paste by combining a little of the milk with the carob powder and sugar, then heat the rest of the milk and add it to the paste.

2. Return the drink to the saucepan and heat it gently until it boils.

Note: This can be whisked briefly to make it frothy, and topped with a little finely grated chocolate, or simply add a dollop of whipped cream. It makes a cheering and nutritious drink for a cold day.

SWEET BANANA SHAKE

Imperial (Metric)	American
1 ripe banana	1 ripe banana
Squeeze of lemon juice	Squeeze of lemon juice
½ pint (¼ litre) milk, (whole, skimmed or soya)	1⅓ cupsful milk (whole, skimmed or soya)
1-2 teaspoonful honey	1-2 teaspoonful honey
1-2 teaspoonsful desiccated coconut	1-2 teaspoonsful desiccated coconut

1. Mash the banana and add the lemon juice.

2. Put all the ingredients into a blender and whisk them well.

Soups

FRENCH ONION SOUP GRATINÉE

Imperial (Metric)
2 large onions
1 oz (25g) polyunsaturated
  margarine
1 pint (½ litre) vegetable stock
Seasoning to taste
2 slices toasted wholemeal bread
1-2 oz (25-50g) grated cheese
  (Gruyère is traditional but Edam
  tastes just as good)

American
2 large onions
2½ tablespoonsful polyunsaturated
  margarine
2½ cupsful vegetable stock
Seasoning to taste
2 slices toasted wholemeal bread
¼-½ cupful grated cheese
  (Gruyère is traditional but Edam
  tastes just as good)

1. Slice the onions into thin rounds and fry them gently in the melted margarine.

2. When the colour begins to turn, add the stock and seasoning, bring to the boil, then simmer gently for 15 minutes.

3. Pour the soup onto the slices of toast in two bowls, sprinkle half the cheese over each, and place under a grill until the cheese begins to brown.

Note: This is a warming, filling soup.

GREEN PEA SOUP

Imperial (Metric)	American
1 tablespoonful vegetable oil	1 tablespoonful vegetable oil
1 leek or 1 onion, finely chopped	1 leek or 1 onion, finely chopped
1/2 teaspoonful yeast extract	1/2 teaspoonful yeast extract
1 pint (1/2 litre) water	2 1/2 cupsful water
4 oz (100g) green split peas, soaked overnight	1/2 cupful green split peas, soaked overnight

1. Heat the oil, then fry the leek or onion until just transparent.

2. Dissolve the yeast extract in the water, then add all the ingredients and simmer gently until the peas are soft.

CAULIFLOWER AND POTATO SOUP

Imperial (Metric)	American
1 pint (1/2 litre) vegetable stock	2 1/2 cupsful vegetable stock
1 oz (25g) polyunsaturated margarine	2 1/2 tablespoonsful polyunsaturated margarine
2 oz (50g) skimmed milk powder	2/3 cupful skimmed milk powder
Seasoning to taste	Seasoning to taste
1/2 small cauliflower, cooked	1/2 small cauliflower, cooked
2 medium potatoes, cooked	2 medium potatoes, cooked
1 medium onion, finely sliced	1 medium onion, finely sliced
Chopped parsley or chives (optional)	Chopped parsley or chives (optional)

1. Heat the stock and add the margarine, milk powder and seasoning.

2. Chop the cauliflower and potato, and put them into the blender with a little of the stock.

3. When smooth, return all the ingredients to the saucepan and simmer with the onion.

4.   Sprinkle with parsley or chives if liked. Serve this soup hot or cold.

Note: Leeks can be used instead of cauliflower when in season.

MISO SOUP

Imperial (Metric)	**American**
1 oz (25g) miso	2½ tablespoonsful miso
1 pint (½ litre) water	2½ cupsful water
4 small carrots, grated	4 small carrots, grated
1 medium onion, sliced	1 medium onion, sliced
1 tablespoonful vegetable oil	1 tablespoonful vegetable oil
Seasoning to taste	Seasoning to taste

1.   Put the miso and water in a saucepan and heat the liquid gently, stirring to dissolve the miso.

2.   Fry the vegetables for a few minutes in the oil.

3.   Add the vegetables to the stock, season well and simmer for about 20 minutes.

MEAL-IN-A-SOUP

Illustrated in colour

Imperial (Metric)	American
½ oz (15g) polyunsaturated margarine	1 tablespoonful polyunsaturated margarine
1 small onion, sliced	1 small onion, sliced
1 oz (25g) red lentils, washed	2 tablespoonsful red lentils, washed
1 stick of celery, chopped	1 stick of celery, chopped
1 large tomato, chopped	1 large tomato, chopped
1 large carrot, chopped	1 large carrot, chopped
½ small green pepper, chopped	½ small green capsicum
¼ small cabbage, chopped	¼ small cabbage, chopped
1 pint (½ litre) water	2½ cupsful water
1 teaspoonful yeast extract	1 teaspoonful yeast extract
Seasoning to taste	Seasoning to taste
1-2 oz (25-50g) grated cheese (optional)	¼-½ cupful grated cheese (optional)

1. Melt the margarine, then gently fry the onion until just changing colour.

2. Add the lentils, vegetables and water to the frying pan.

3. When boiling, stir in the yeast extract, season and leave to simmer for about 30 minutes. Although this soup is already a nutritionally balanced meal, you can boost the protein by topping it with grated cheese just before serving.

Note: The vegetables can also be varied according to what is in season. Mushrooms, courgettes and cauliflower taste especially good.

BROCCOLI RICE SOUP

Imperial (Metric)	**American**
¾ lb (350g) broccoli, fresh or frozen	¾ lb broccoli, fresh or frozen
¾ lb (350g) potatoes, peeled and diced	¾ lb potatoes, peeled and diced
1 medium onion, sliced	1 medium onion, sliced
1 pint (½ litre) vegetable stock	2½ cupsful vegetable stock
1 oz (25g) polyunsaturated margarine or butter	2½ tablespoonsful polyunsaturated margarine or butter
1-2 oz (25-50g) brown rice	¼ cupful brown rice
Seasoning to taste	Seasoning to taste
Grated cheese (optional)	Grated cheese (optional)

1. Trim the broccoli, removing any blemishes and tough stems, then break it into florets.

2. Place the broccoli in a large saucepan with the potatoes, onion and stock, bring it to the boil, then cover and simmer for about 30 minutes or until the vegetables are soft.

3. *Purée* the soup in a blender, then return it to the pan.

4. Add the margarine and rice to the soup, and cook it gently for 15-20 minutes, until the rice is cooked but not mushy.

5. Season to taste and serve as it is or with some grated cheese to make it even more of a meal.

BEAN CHOWDER

Imperial (Metric)	American
4 oz (100g) haricot beans (or tinned baked beans)	½ cupful haricot beans (or tinned baked beans)
1 tablespoonful vegetable oil	1 tablespoonful vegetable oil
1 large onion, sliced	1 large onion, sliced
1 pint (½ litre) vegetable stock	2½ cupsful vegetable stock
3 tablespoonsful tomato purée	3½ tablespoonsful tomato purée
Good pinch of raw cane sugar	Good pinch of raw cane sugar
Good pinch of dry mustard	Good pinch of dry mustard
Seasoning to taste	Seasoning to taste
Parsley or soya 'Bacon' bits to garnish	Parsley or soya 'Bacon' bits to garnish

1. Soak the beans overnight in water if necessary, then put them into a saucepan with fresh water and cook them gently until soft. (As it's hardly worth spending so long cooking such a small amount, cook extra to use another time, or make this soup when you have some beans left over from a previous meal.)

2. Heat the oil in another saucepan and gently *sauté* the onion.

3. Add the stock, tomato *purée*, sugar and mustard and cook for 10 minutes.

4. Add the drained haricot beans and heat them through.

5. Serve this soup with plenty of fresh parsley or in the traditional way with 'bacon' bits scattered on top.

PARSNIP SOUP WITH WALNUTS

Imperial (Metric)	American
1 lb (1/2 kilo) parsnips	1 lb parsnips
1 large onion	1 large onion
1 large carrot	1 large carrot
1 oz (25g) polyunsaturated margarine or butter	2 1/2 tablespoonsful polyunsaturated margarine or butter
1 pint (1/2 litre) vegetable stock	2 1/2 cupsful vegetable stock
2 tablespoonsful single cream or natural yogurt	2 1/2 tablespoonsful single cream or natural yogurt
1 oz (25g) walnuts, chopped	1/4 cupful chopped English walnuts
Seasoning to taste	Seasoning to taste

1. Peel the vegetables and chop them into small pieces.

2. *Sauté* them briefly in the melted margarine before adding them to the vegetable stock and bringing to the boil.

3. Cover and simmer for 30 minutes or until tender.

4. *Purée* the vegetables in a blender or press them through a sieve.

5. Return the *purée* to the saucepan and stir in the cream or yogurt, then heat the soup through very gently — it must not be allowed to boil.

6. Sprinkle with the walnuts just before eating.

COOK NOW, EAT LATER

One of the things that puts many people off the idea of taking a packed lunch is the preparation involved. Keeping your lunches interesting means planning in advance. You can, of course, simply throw whatever is handy into a bag as you race out of the front door, but that method is unlikely to result in an interesting, nutritionally balanced meal. More likely you will end up taking cheese sandwiches every day — and that is enough to send anyone rushing to the nearest Steak House!

Using Left-overs
A clever way to cut preparation time whilst adding variety to your packed lunch is to use left-over portions of something you have previously eaten hot. It's amazing how good many cooked dishes taste when cold! Heat can tend to dull the more subtle ingredients — the tastes of herbs, the milder spices, or garden-fresh vegetables are often completely lost in a hot dish. When the dish is eaten cold, however, these tastes can be enjoyed to the full.

You will, of course, have to make sure you have enough ingredients to cook more than you need for your evening meal — and enough will-power not to finish the whole lot at one sitting! Simply cut off and put aside the portion you intend to take for lunch before you serve the hot dish. With some recipes you can actually cook your portion separately, although at the same time. Put an individual serving of the prepared ingredients in a small foil dish, cook, then when it has cooled down, cover it with more foil and put in the refrigerator. Come the morning, your packed lunch is virtually ready, with the minimum of time and effort.

The recipes given here all contain simple but wholesome ingredients, are quick and easy to prepare, and taste delicious both hot and cold. Do try using other cooked dishes as part of your packed lunch too. Providing that the basic ingredients are fresh and nutritious, and that the food has not been left in the refrigerator long enough to go stale, you will undoubtedly enjoy discovering more 'new' tastes than you imagined possible.

PIZZA-IN-A-PANIC

For base:

Imperial (Metric)	American
2 oz (50g) polyunsaturated margarine	¼ cupful polyunsaturated margarine
½ lb (¼ kilo) plain wholemeal flour	2 cupsful plain wholemeal flour
¼ pint (150ml) milk	⅔ cupful milk

For topping:

Imperial (Metric)	American
2 tablespoonsful vegetable oil	2½ tablespoonsful vegetable oil
2 large onions, sliced	2 large onions, sliced
½ lb (¼ kilo) tomatoes, sliced	½ lb tomatoes, sliced
5 oz (125g) cheese (bel paese is traditional, but any hard cheese will do)	1¼ cupsful grated cheese (bel paese is traditional, but any hard cheese will do)
4 oz (100g) mushrooms, sliced	1½ cupsful sliced mushrooms
Olives (optional)	Olives (optional)
Seasoning and herbs to taste	Seasoning and herbs to taste

1. Rub the margarine into the flour, season and pour the milk into the centre, mixing to make a soft dough.

2. Turn the dough on to a floured board and knead it lightly, then divide it and shape it into two rounds.

3. Roll each round to a thickness of about half an inch, place them on greased baking sheets and brush with oil.

4. Heat the oil and gently fry the sliced onions, then spread them over the pizzas.

5. Top with the tomatoes and thinly sliced or grated cheese, followed by the mushrooms.

6. Stone and halve the olives and spread them over the top with a little extra grated cheese, some herbs and a very small amount of oil.

7. Bake for 25-30 minutes at 400°F/200°C (Gas Mark 6).

Note: An alternative is to make a cheese sauce and pour that over the tomatoes; top with mushrooms, herbs and a sprinkling of cheese and bake as above. (Both these pizzas taste just as good as the true Italian pizza, but take half the time to prepare!)

MEATLESS SCOTCH EGGS

Imperial (Metric)	American
1 oz (25g) plain wholemeal flour	¼ cupful plain wholemeal flour
3 oz (75g) cheese, finely grated	¾ cupful finely grated cheese
1 egg	1 egg
Seasoning to taste	Seasoning to taste
Milk to bind	Milk to bind
2 hard-boiled eggs, shelled	2 hard-boiled eggs, shelled
Wholemeal breadcrumbs	Wholemeal breadcrumbs

1. Mix together the flour, cheese, egg and seasoning.

2. Add enough milk to make the mixture a fairly stiff consistency.

3. Divide the mixture into two and roll it around the eggs (this is easier with damp fingers).

4. Coat the eggs evenly in breadcrumbs and deep-fry them in hot vegetable fat for approximately 2 minutes, or until a golden brown colour.

5. Drain the eggs before serving.

Note: You can also make meatless scotch eggs by using one of the many nut rissole mixes in packets available at health food shops. Usually made from a basic mixture of nuts and wheat, they provide a good source of protein without cholesterol.

BEAN BURGERS

Imperial (Metric)	American
4 oz (100g) dried beans (any kind — try butter beans and black-eyed peas first)	½ cupful dried beans (any kind — try Lima beans and black-eyed peas first)
1 stick of celery, finely chopped	1 stick of celery, finely chopped
1 onion, finely chopped	1 onion, finely chopped
2 tablespoonsful vegetable oil	2½ tablespoonsful vegetable oil
Squeeze of lemon juice	Squeeze of lemon juice
Sprig of parsley, chopped	Sprig of parsley, chopped
Seasoning to taste	Seasoning to taste
4 oz (100g) rolled oats or wholemeal breadcrumbs	1 cupful rolled oats or wholemeal breadcrumbs
Wholemeal flour	Wholemeal flour

1. Soak the beans overnight, then cook them until soft (if you're in a hurry, you could use tinned beans instead).

2. Drain the beans then mash them thoroughly.

3. Cook the celery and onion in the oil until they begin to soften, then combine all the ingredients together well.

4. Shape the mixture into five burgers, coat them with the flour, and shallow-fry them until golden.

5. Serve four immediately with a bubbly cheese sauce and lightly cooked green vegetables. Take the extra one as part of your packed lunch — tuck it into a soft wholemeal roll, and eat it with some crisp, fresh cole-slaw.

CHEESE SAVOURY SLICE

Imperial (Metric)	American
4 oz (100g) Cheddar cheese	1 cupful grated Cheddar cheese
2 large carrots	2 large carrots
1 small onion	1 small onion
½ green pepper	½ green capsicum
1 egg	1 egg
2 oz (50g) polyunsaturated margarine	¼ cupful polyunsaturated margarine
5 oz (125g) rolled oats	1¼ cupsful rolled oats
Seasoning and herbs to taste	Seasoning and herbs to taste

1. Finely grate the cheese, carrots, onion and pepper.

2. Beat the egg and melt the margarine, then mix all the ingredients together, making sure they are well blended.

3. Press the mixture into a greased Swiss roll tin and bake at 375°F/190°C (Gas Mark 5) for 20 minutes.

4. Cut into slices and eat half of it hot with a spicy tomato sauce; save the rest to take cold with your packed lunch.

PAELLA

Imperial (Metric)	American
6 oz (150g) brown rice	¾ cupful brown rice
3 tablespoonsful vegetable oil	3½ tablespoonsful vegetable oil
1 small tin pineapple chunks in their own juice	1 small tin pineapple chunks in their own juice
Water	Water
1 small green pepper, sliced	1 small green capsicum, sliced
4 oz (100g) mushrooms, sliced	1½ cupsful sliced mushrooms
2 oz (50g) sultanas	⅓ cupful golden seedless raisins
2 oz (50g) peanuts	3½ tablespoonsful peanuts
3 tablespoonsful tomato purée	3½ tablespoonsful tomato purée

1. Cook the rice in the oil until golden, then make up the juice from the tin of pineapple to ¾ pint (400ml) with water. Add this to the rice, then cover the pan.

2. Simmer gently until the rice has absorbed the liquid.

3. Meanwhile fry the green pepper and mushrooms, and add them to the cooked rice with all the other ingredients except the pineapple.

4. After heating them through, add the pineapple chunks.

Note: This recipe makes three servings. Share it with someone when freshly cooked, then pop the remainder into the refrigerator to take to work in a polythene container a day or two later.

CREAMY PEAS PASTIES

Illustrated in colour
For shortcrust pastry:

Imperial (Metric)	American
Pinch of sea salt	Pinch of sea salt
6 oz (150g) plain wholemeal flour	1½ cupsful plain wholemeal flour
3 oz (75g) polyunsaturated margarine	7½ tablespoonsful polyunsaturated margarine
1 tablespoonful cold water	1 tablespoonful cold water

3. Creamy Pea Pasties (page 64) and Apple Turnovers (page 108) add interest to Dad's healthy lunchbox.

4. All the energy needed for the sporting life, packed into a tasty bowl of Bulgur Salad with Nuts (page 74).

5. A satisfying slimmer's lunch of Hot Rice-stuffed Tomatoes (page 88) served with mixed green salad.

6. A lunchtime party treat of Marmalade Cake (page 110) and Banana Tea Cake (page 112).

For filling:

Imperial (Metric)	**American**
1 oz (25g) polyunsaturated margarine	2½ tablespoonsful polyunsaturated margarine
1 oz (25g) plain wholemeal flour	¼ cupful plain wholemeal flour
½ pint (¼ litre) milk	1⅓ cupsful milk
4 oz (100g) peas, fresh or frozen	¾ cupful peas, fresh or frozen
Seasoning to taste	Seasoning to taste

1. Add the salt to the flour, then rub in the margarine until the mix resembles fine breadcrumbs.

2. Gradually blend in the water with a fork until a soft, rather wet dough is formed. Knead the dough a little, then leave it to stand. (As wholemeal flour makes pastry more crumbly, you can make it easier to roll out by first wrapping the dough in cling foil and putting it in the refrigerator for at least 30 minutes.)

3. Turn the dough onto a floured board, roll it out thinly and use a saucer to cut it into rounds.

4. Meanwhile, heat the margarine and cook the flour in it gently for a few minutes.

5. Remove the saucepan from the heat and add the milk, stirring it to prevent lumps forming, then return the sauce to the heat and stir again until it thickens. Season to taste.

6. Cook and drain the peas and add them to the white sauce.

7. Place a generous portion of the mixture onto each round of dough, fold them in half and press the edges together.

8. Place the pasties on a greased baking sheet, and cook for 20-30 minutes at 400°F/200°C (Gas Mark 6).

HERB-TOMATO FLAN

For flan:

Imperial (Metric)	American
Pinch of sea salt	Pinch of sea salt
6 oz (150g) wholemeal flour	1½ cupful wholemeal flour
3 oz (75g) polyunsaturated margarine	7½ tablespoonsful polyunsaturated margarine
1 tablespoonful cold water	1 tablespoonful cold water

For filling:

Imperial (Metric)	American
2 oz (50g) polyunsaturated margarine	¼ cupful polyunsaturated margarine
1 medium onion, sliced	1 medium onion, sliced
1 small pepper, sliced	1 small pepper, sliced
1 lb (½ kilo) tomatoes, peeled and chopped	1 lb tomatoes, peeled and chopped
1-2 teaspoonsful mixed herbs	1-2 teaspoonsful mixed herbs
Seasoning to taste	Seasoning to taste
2 eggs	2 eggs
⅓ pint (200ml) milk	¾ cupful milk
4 oz (100g) cheese (cottage or grated Cheddar)	1 cupful cheese (cottage or grated Cheddar)
2 tablespoonsful tomato purée	2½ tablespoonsful tomato purée

1. Prepare a shortcrust pastry (see page 65) and use it to line a flan dish.

2. Melt the margarine, *sauté* the onion and pepper until soft and add the tomatoes.

3. Sprinkle with the herbs and seasoning and cover, then leave the mixture to simmer for a few minutes.

4. Mash the tomatoes and continue cooking uncovered until a thick *purée* is formed. Set the mixture aside to cool.

5. Beat the eggs, add the milk and grated cheese and finally the tomato *purée*.

6. Blend the mixture thoroughly, adjust the seasoning and pour it into the flan case.

7. Add a final sprinkling of grated cheese if liked and cook at 350°F/180°C (Gas Mark 4) for 30 minutes.

Note: This is an unusual flan that is especially satisfying. Its firm texture makes it a good choice for a packed lunch.

BRAZILIAN LOAF

Imperial (Metric)	American
1 medium onion, chopped	1 medium onion, chopped
2 tablespoonsful vegetable oil	2½ tablespoonsful vegetable oil
4 oz (100g) Brazil nuts, chopped	¾ cupful chopped Brazil nuts
1 tablespoonful wheatgerm (optional)	1 tablespoonful wheatgerm (optional)
Seasoning to taste	Seasoning to taste
Herbs to taste	Herbs to taste
1 egg	1 egg
Wholemeal breadcrumbs	Wholemeal breadcrumbs

1. Fry the onion in the oil until transparent.

2. Grind the nuts and mix them with the onion, wheatgerm, seasoning and herbs.

3. Beat the egg and add it to the mixture with enough breadcrumbs to make it fairly firm.

4. Turn the mixture into a greased tin, dot with polyunsaturated margarine, and bake at 350°F/180°C (Gas Mark 4) for 30 minutes.

Note: Brazilian Loaf tastes good with a brown (non-meat) gravy when hot. When cold, eat it with salad, or sliced thinly in sandwiches.

MILLET AND VEGETABLE CROQUETTES

Imperial (Metric)	American
4 oz (100g) millet	1/2 cupful millet
1/2-3/4 cupful mixed cooked vegetables	3/4 cupful mixed cooked vegetables
2 oz (50g) plain wholemeal flour	1/2 cupful plain wholemeal flour
Soy sauce	Soy sauce
Seasoning to taste	Seasoning to taste
Vegetable oil for frying	Vegetable oil for frying

1. Cook the millet according to instructions on the packet (or use millet as part of your evening meal and allow some extra for the croquettes). Set it aside to cool.

2. Chop the vegetables up small and add them to the millet with the flour, soy sauce and seasoning, blending well to give a firm consistency.

3. Divide the mixture into croquettes, roll them in a little extra flour, and deep-fry them. Drain well before leaving them to cool.

Note: This recipe is an ideal way to use up left-overs. You can use rice instead of millet, and can add an egg or some cheese for a change.

RATATOUILLE

Imperial (Metric)	American
4 tomatoes	4 tomatoes
2 large onions	2 large onions
1 lb (½ kilo) marrow or courgettes (or one cucumber)	1 lb summer squash or zucchini (or one cucumber)
2 large aubergines	2 large eggplants
1 small green pepper	1 small green capsicum
6 tablespoonsful vegetable oil	7½ tablespoonsful vegetable oil
Seasoning to taste	Seasoning to taste
1 clove of garlic, crushed (or garlic salt)	1 clove of garlic, crushed (or garlic salt)
1 small tin sweet corn	1 small tin sweet corn
Grated cheese (optional)	Grated cheese (optional)

1. Skin and slice the tomatoes, onions, marrow (or courgettes or cucumber).

2. Chop the aubergines and green pepper, heat the oil and add all the prepared vegetables, seasoning and garlic.

3. Stir well, cover the saucepan and simmer for 30-45 minutes. (If the oven is alight you can cook your ratatouille on the bottom shelf — keep it covered and make sure the vegetables have plenty of liquid to cook in.)

4. When almost cooked, open the tin of sweet corn, drain it and stir it into the ratatouille. Reurn to the heat.

Note: The sweet corn provides some protein, but if you intend to take cold ratatouille for lunch and want to boost the protein, put a portion of the vegetables into a small foil dish, top with grated cheese and put it under the grill to melt the cheese.

PASTA SALAD

Imperial (Metric)	American
1½-2 oz (40-50g) wholewheat pasta shells	1 cupful wholewheat pasta shells
2 sticks of celery	2 sticks of celery
1 spring onion	1 scallion
2 tablespoonsful mayonnaise	2½ tablespoonsful mayonnaise
2 tablespoonsful natural yogurt	2½ tablespoonsful natural yogurt
Seasoning to taste	Seasoning to taste
A few black olives	A few black olives
Fresh parsley, chopped	Fresh parsley, chopped
1 hard-boiled egg, roughly chopped	1 hard-boiled egg, roughly chopped

1. Drop the pasta shells into a saucepan of boiling water and cook for about 10 minutes or until the pasta is tender but not over-cooked.

2. Drain the pasta, rinse with cold water, and drain again.

3. Cut the celery into small pieces, and also the onion.

4. Mix together the mayonnaise and yogurt, and season the dressing well.

5. Combine the pasta with the celery, onion, olives, parsley and enough dressing to moisten (you may not need as much as you have prepared — it depends on your personal taste).

6. Serve topped with the chopped egg.

Note: This makes one very generous portion.

STUFFED COURGETTES

Imperial (Metric)	American
4 medium courgettes	4 medium zucchini
½ oz (15g) polyunsaturated margarine	1 tablespoonful polyunsaturated margarine
1 small onion, chopped	1 small onion, chopped
1 oz (25g) wholemeal breadcrumbs	½ cupful wholemeal breadcrumbs
Fresh parsley, chopped	Fresh parsley, chopped
2 oz (50g) Cheddar cheese, grated	½ cupful grated Cheddar cheese
1 oz (25g) walnuts, chopped	¼ cupful English walnuts, chopped

1. Wash, dry and trim the ends of the courgettes, then cut them in half lengthwise.

2. Remove most of the pulp, being careful not to break the skins.

3. Simmer the courgette shells in boiling water for about 5 minutes, then drain them well and arrange them cut-side up in a lightly greased ovenproof dish.

4. Melt the margarine and fry the onion until it begins to colour, then add the courgette pulp chopped into small pieces, and the breadcrumbs. Cook for 5 minutes or so over a low heat.

5. Stir in the parsley, season to taste, and add most of the cheese.

6. Pile the mixture into the courgette shells, and top them with the rest of the cheese and a sprinkling of nuts.

7. Bake the courgettes at 375°F/190°C (Gas Mark 5) for 30-40 minutes, or until the flesh is cooked. (As this is really enough for 4 small portions, you could eat half of it straight away and save the rest for another day. Pack it into a small metal foil container and cover with cling foil to carry.)

Note: All sorts of ingredients can be used in this recipe. If, for example, you have no nuts handy, substitute a few cooked peas or sweet corn kernels as part of the mixture, and save some of the breadcrumbs for a crispy topping. An egg can be added to the filling for increased protein, or a little mashed tofu.

'SAUSAGE' ROLLS

For puff pastry:

Imperial (Metric)
4 oz (100g) plain wholemeal flour
Pinch of sea salt
Squeeze of lemon juice
Water to mix
4 oz (100g) polyunsaturated
    margarine or butter

American
1 cupful plain wholemeal flour
Pinch of sea salt
Squeeze of lemon juice
Water to mix
½ cupful polyunsaturated
    margarine or butter

For filling:

Imperial (Metric)
1 tin or packet of 'sausage' nut mix
1 egg, beaten or water

American
1 tin or pack of 'sausage' nut mix
1 egg, beaten or water

1. Place the flour in a bowl and add the salt, lemon juice, and just enough water to make a soft dough.

2. On a floured board, roll the dough out to an oblong.

3. Cut the fat into small pieces and dot them over the centre third of the dough.

4. Fold one third over to cover the fat, then the other third and seal the edges. Turn the dough and roll it out to an oblong again.

5. Repeat this process of rolling and folding the dough seven times, wrapping it in cling film and putting it in the fridge for 10 minutes at least between each rolling. (The results will, in fact, be better if you work in a cool room with cool hands and utensils!)

6. Either cut or shape the sausages into eight 2 in. pieces.

7. Roll half the prepared pastry to a strip about 2 in. wide and place the sausages along it, then cover them with another strip of pastry.

8. Dampen the edges either with egg or water and press them down firmly, then cut between the sausages and also seal these new edges.

9. Make one or two slits on the top of each roll, and brush — if liked — with more egg. Place the rolls on a baking tray and bake at 425°F/220°C (Gas Mark 7) for about 20 minutes or until the pastry is cooked. (These may be eaten hot or cold.)

Note: As puff pastry is a rather complicated process, it might be worth making extra and keeping it in the freezer to use on another occasion. You can, of course, use shortcrust pastry for different, but equally tasty sausage rolls.

BULGUR SALAD WITH NUTS

Illustrated in colour

Imperial (Metric)	American
Approx. 2 tablespoonsful vegetable oil	Approx. 2½ tablespoonsful vegetable oil
4 oz (100g) bulgur (cracked wheat)	⅔ cupful bulgur (cracked wheat)
¼ pint (150ml) water	⅔ cupful water
1 small onion, chopped	1 small onion, chopped
½ clove of garlic, crushed	½ clove of garlic, crushed
1 teaspoonful lemon juice	1 teaspoonful lemon juice
Fresh parsley, chopped	Fresh parsley, chopped
Fresh mint, chopped	Fresh mint, chopped
Seasoning to taste	Seasoning to taste
½ small red or green pepper	½ small red or green capsicum
2 oz (50g) chopped nuts	½ cupful chopped nuts

1. Heat the oil in a saucepan and gently *sauté* the bulgur, stirring frequently, for a few minutes.

2. Add the water and cook the bulgur, covered, for about 15 minutes, or until the grains are tender but not soggy. (You may need to add a tiny drop more water.)

3. When cooked, drain any excess water from the bulgur, then transfer it to a bowl.

4. Stir in the onion, garlic, lemon juice, parsley and mint, plus the seasoning. (If the mixture seems to need it, add a drop more oil.)

5. Cut the pepper into rings and arrange them on top with a sprinkling of the nuts.

HOT SNACKS FOR THE HOUSEWIFE

Ridiculous as it may seem, the one person who has access to a selection of foods, and facilities to prepare and cook them, is often the one who eats least — or least well! — at lunch times.

The housewife, or anyone who is housebound most weekdays, tends to pick at bits, but never actually sits down and enjoys her food! A few biscuits, a slice of cake, perhaps a chocolate bar or a handful of salted peanuts . . . it's the kind of eating pattern that can leave you feeling hungry — and weighing heavy! It can also lead to nutritional deficiencies. Amazingly, it's quite possible for someone who is fat to be starved of certain vital nutrients.

Excuses for not eating a proper lunch are many: it's not worth cooking for one; it takes too much time; you are never hungry midday; you do not like to eat alone; the baby needs attention. Be that as it may, it is important that everyone who leads a busy life should provide their bodies with the fuel needed to keep them going. The woman who is too tired to eat a proper lunch would undoubtedly feel much less tired if she made the effort!

Soup and Salad Lunch
An easy solution to the problem is the soup and salad lunch. Make a big pot of soup early in the week and heat up a portion as needed. Whilst it is cooking, prepare a salad with whatever ingredients you have handy. This kind of lunch can be as light or as hearty, as expensive or as thrifty as you choose.

Alternatively, try some of the hot snacks given here. Most of them can be prepared in a very short space of time. You can eat them alone, or add crispbread, toast, potatoes, left-over rice, grated cheese, nuts, whatever you fancy to make them into a more filling meal. Unless otherwise stated, recipes are for one portion, but can easily be increased if you're having company to lunch.

BEAN HOTPOT

Imperial (Metric)	American
1 small green pepper	1 small green capsicum
1 small onion	1 small onion
1 tomato	1 tomato
1 small tin baked beans	1 small tin baked beans
Seasoning to taste	Seasoning to taste

1. Chop the vegetables and combine them with the beans and their sauce.

2. Season to taste and place the mixture in a saucepan, cover, and simmer gently for about 15 minutes. Eat this with a salad or on toast.

EGGBURGER

Imperial (Metric)	American
1 soft wholemeal roll	1 soft wholemeal roll
1 egg	1 egg
2 tablespoonsful vegetable oil	2½ tablespoonsful vegetable oil
Tomato purée (optional)	Tomato purée (optional)

1. Slice and lightly toast the cut surfaces of the wholemeal roll.

2. Fry the egg gently in hot oil, then turn it and cook the other side.

3. Spread the tomato *purée* on one half of the roll, top with the egg, and sandwich with the other half. Eat this, American style, with a tangy relish.

MUSHROOMS PAPRIKA ON TOAST

Imperial (Metric)	American
3 oz (75g) mushrooms	1½ cupsful mushrooms
½ oz (15g) polyunsaturated margarine	1 tablespoonful polyunsaturated margarine
¼ pint (150ml) milk	⅔ cupful milk
1 tablespoonful skimmed milk powder	1 tablespoonful skimmed milk powder
1 teaspoonful paprika	1 teaspoonful paprika
2 slices wholemeal bread, lightly toasted	2 slices wholemeal bread, lightly toasted

1. Wash and slice the mushrooms.

2. Heat the margarine in a saucepan, and add the milk into which has been stirred the skimmed milk powder and paprika.

3. Drop the mushrooms into the liquid, cover, and cook on a low heat for 5 minutes.

4. Serve on the toast.

Note: The skimmed milk powder adds extra protein to this delicious snack.

QUICK MACARONI CHEESE

Imperial (Metric)
1 pint (½ litre) water
1 stick of celery, chopped
1½-2 oz (40-50g) wholewheat
   macaroni
2 oz (50g) cream cheese
Seasoning to taste

American
2½ cupsful water
1 stick of celery, chopped
¼-½ cupful wholewheat
   macaroni
¼ cupful cream cheese
Seasoning to taste

1. Bring the water to the boil. Add the chopped celery and macaroni, and cook for about 10 minutes or until the macaroni is soft.

2. Strain the macaroni and return it to the saucepan with the cream cheese.

3. Stir the mixture over a very low heat until the cheese has melted into a creamy sauce.

4. Season and eat at once.

LEEKS PROVENCAL

Imperial (Metric)
2 leeks
2 tablespoonsful vegetable oil
2 tomatoes (or tinned equivalent)
Squeeze of lemon juice
Seasoning to taste
1 egg

American
2 leeks
2½ tablespoonsful vegetable oil
2 tomatoes (or tinned equivalent)
Squeeze of lemon juice
Seasoning to taste
1 egg

1. Wash and chop the leeks into small pieces.

2. Cook them gently in the oil for a few minutes, turning them occasionally, then add the chopped tomatoes, lemon juice and seasoning.

3. Simmer the mixture for 5 minutes and, meanwhile, boil the egg lightly.

4. When the leeks are ready, pour them onto a plate and top with the sliced egg.

POTATO AND PEA RISSOLES

Imperial (Metric)	American
2 medium potatoes, cooked	2 medium potatoes, cooked
2 oz (50g) cheese, grated	½ cupful grated cheese
1 heaped tablespoonful peas, mashed	1 heaped tablespoonful peas, mashed
Wholemeal flour to mix	Wholemeal flour to mix
Seasoning to taste	Seasoning to taste
2 tablespoonsful vegetable oil	2½ tablespoonsful vegetable oil

1. Mash the potatoes well, then add the grated cheese and blend it in well.

2. Stir in the peas, and if the mixture is not firm enough to shape into rissoles, add a little flour.

3. Shape the mixture into rissoles, dip them in the flour and shallow-fry them until crisp. Serve these with a salad.

NUTTY RAREBIT

Imperial (Metric)	American
2-3 oz (50-75g) cheese, grated	1/2-3/4 cupful grated cheese
1 oz (25g) chopped nuts	1/4 cupful chopped nuts
Seasoning to taste	Seasoning to taste
Milk to mix	Milk to mix
2 slices wholemeal bread, lightly toasted	2 slices wholemeal bread, lightly toasted

1. Mix the cheese, nuts and seasoning together, then add a little milk to give a smoother, creamier consistency.

2. Spread the mixture on the two pieces of toast, and cook under a hot grill until brown and bubbly. (A tomato and chicory salad makes a good accompaniment.)

SLIMMER'S SPAGHETTI

Imperial (Metric)	American
1 pint (1/2 litre) water	2 1/2 cupsful water
2 oz (50g) wholewheat spaghetti	2 oz wholewheat spaghetti
2 tablespoonsful vegetable oil	2 1/2 tablespoonsful vegetable oil
2 tomatoes, chopped	2 tomatoes, chopped
1 large onion, chopped	1 large onion, chopped
2 oz (50g) mushrooms, chopped	3/4 cupful chopped mushrooms
Seasoning to taste	Seasoning to taste
Parmesan cheese (optional)	Parmesan cheese (optional)

1. Heat the water, add the spaghetti, and cook it for about 10 minutes until soft.

2. Meanwhile, heat the oil in a frying pan and add the chopped vegetables. (If the mixture is too dry you may need to add a little extra water.)

3. Simmer for 5 minutes, season, and serve over cooked spaghetti.

4. Sprinkle with Parmesan cheese if desired.

CHEESE AND ONION CRISPIES

Imperial (Metric)	American
1 large onion, sliced	1 large onion, sliced
2 tablespoonsful vegetable oil	2 1/2 tablespoonsful vegetable oil
3 wholewheat crispbreads	3 wholewheat crispbreads or Graham crackers
3 oz (75g) cheese, finely grated	3/4 cupful finely grated cheese

1. Lightly fry the onion in the oil and divide it between the crispbreads.

2. Top each crispbread with a portion of cheese and pop them under the grill for just a few minutes until the cheese melts.

VEGETABLES IN HOLLANDAISE SAUCE

For sauce:

Imperial (Metric)	American
2 tablespoonsful polyunsaturated margarine or butter	2½ tablespoonsful polyunsaturated margarine or butter
3 tablespoonsful wholemeal flour	3½ tablespoonsful wholemeal flour
¾ pint (400ml) water	2 cupsful water
Seasoning to taste	Seasoning to taste
1 tablespoonful milk or cream	1 tablespoonful milk or cream
1 egg yolk	1 egg yolk
1 tablespoonful lemon juice	1 tablespoonful lemon juice
Tarragon to taste	Tarragon to taste

For vegetable base:

Imperial (Metric)	American
1 carrot	1 carrot
¼ small cauliflower	¼ small cauliflower
1 onion	1 onion
1 tablespoonful peas	1 tablespoonful peas
(or your choice of mixed vegetables — broccoli and Brussels sprouts go well with this sauce)	(or your choice of mixed vegetables — broccoli and Brussels sprouts go well with this sauce)

1. To make the sauce, heat one teaspoonful of the margarine, add it to the flour and cook until brown.

2. Pour in the water and cook for a few minutes longer.

3. Dissolve the rest of the margarine in the hot water, add seasoning and remove the saucepan from the heat.

4. Mix together the milk and egg yolk. Add the lemon juice to the water, then the egg mixture, stirring slowly all the time so the egg does not curdle.

5. Sprinkle in a little tarragon and pour the sauce over the cooked, hot vegetables.

Note: This makes a generous portion, so let the extra serving cool, and reheat it very gently over hot, not boiling water when you need it. It also tastes delicious served at room temperature with a cold asparagus or green bean salad, or with battered, deep-fried mushrooms.

ORIENTAL CABBAGE

Imperial (Metric)	American
2 tablespoonsful vegetable oil	2½ tablespoonsful vegetable oil
1 small cabbage heart, shredded	1 small cabbage heart, shredded
2 oz (50g) mushrooms, sliced	¾ cupful sliced mushrooms
½ teaspoonful yeast extract	½ teaspoonful yeast extract
1 tablespoonful hot water	1 tablespoonful hot water
2 teaspoonsful soy sauce	2 teaspoonsful soy sauce
Seasoning to taste	Seasoning to taste
1 teaspoonful raw cane sugar	1 teaspoonful raw cane sugar
1 oz (25g) almond flakes	¼ cupful almond flakes

1. Heat the oil, add the cabbage and mushrooms, and cook for 5 minutes over a medium heat, turning frequently.

2. Dissolve the yeast extract in the hot water and pour it over the vegetables together with the soy sauce, seasoning and sugar.

3. Cook for 5 minutes more, then add the almonds and serve.

Note: This is a light dish that is usually served as part of a meal (with brown rice etc.), but it is crunchy and flavoursome, so that it can be enjoyed on its own. (If you want something more filling, add some potatoes, a few crisps, or a slice or two of wholemeal toast.)

DHALL

Imperial (Metric)	American
1 pint (½ litre) water	2½ cupsful water
¼ teaspoonful ginger	¼ teaspoonful ginger
¼ teaspoonful turmeric	¼ teaspoonful turmeric
Pinch of sea salt	Pinch of sea salt
4 oz (100g) red lentils	½ cupful red lentils
1 onion, chopped	1 onion, chopped
1 teaspoonful garam masala	1 teaspoonful garam masala
½ oz (15g) polyunsaturated margarine	1 tablespoonful polyunsaturated margarine
½ teaspoonful caraway seeds	½ teaspoonful caraway seeds
Squeeze of lemon juice	Squeeze of lemon juice
Seasoning to taste	Seasoning to taste

1. Bring the water to the boil, add the ginger, turmeric, salt and lentils.

2. Simmer gently for about 30 minutes, until the lentils can be easily mashed, then drain them.

3. Meanwhile, fry the onion and garam masala in the margarine. Add the seeds and cook them for a few minutes.

4. Remove the saucepan from the heat and add the lemon juice and seasoning to the lentils. Blend well and eat immediately.

Note: Traditionally this Indian dish is eaten with rice and vegetables. Alternatively, it may be eaten with a crisp salad. The amount given here is probably more than you can manage at one sitting, in which case keep the left-over portion in the refrigerator and reheat it another day — it will be all the better for having been around long enough for the flavours to blend and mature.

MARROW MORNAY

Imperial (Metric)	American
½ medium-sized marrow	½ medium-sized summer squash
½ oz (15g) polyunsaturated margarine	1 tablespoonful polyunsaturated margarine
½ oz (15g) wholemeal flour	1 tablespoonful wholemeal flour
¼ pint (150ml) milk	⅔ cupful milk
2 oz (50g) cheese, grated	½ cupful grated cheese
2 tablespoonsful wholemeal breadcrumbs	2½ tablespoonsful wholemeal breadcrumbs

1. Peel the marrow, cut it into rounds, and discard the seeds if tough.

2. Cook the marrow for 5-10 minutes in just enough salted water to cover the rounds (or, better still, steam the marrow until tender).

3. Heat the margarine in a separate saucepan, add the flour and cook until it browns.

4. Pour in the milk and continue stirring until the sauce thickens, then stir in most of the grated cheese.

5. Drain the marrow well, lay it on a plate and cover it with the cheese sauce.

6. Sprinkle the breadcrumbs and remaining cheese over the top and place the dish under a hot grill until the breadcrumbs are crisp and crunchy.

Note: This is a tasty way to dish up low-calorie marrow, which can be a little bland on its own. You can, of course, substitute any other vegetable in season for the marrow.

CREAMY BROAD BEANS

Imperial (Metric)	American
2-3 oz (50-75g) broad beans	1/3-1/2 cupful Windsor beans
2 tablespoonsful vegetable oil	2 1/2 tablespoonsful vegetable oil
1 oz (25g) wholemeal flour	1/4 cupful wholemeal flour
2 oz (50g) skimmed milk powder	2/3 cupful skimmed milk powder
1/2 pint (1/4 litre) water	1 2/3 cupsful water
1 sprig of parsley, chopped	1 sprig of parsley, chopped

1. Cook the beans until tender. (Obviously, fresh beans are better, but if you're in a hurry, use frozen or tinned — they still have a lot of food value to offer.)

2. Heat the oil, add the flour and cook it gently.

3. Mix the milk powder into the water (you can use the water in which the beans were cooked for extra flavour), then pour the liquid into the flour.

4. Mix well, bring to the boil, then stir to keep the sauce smooth.

5. Drain the beans and add them to the sauce, making sure they are all covered.

6. Stir in the parsley and cook for a minute or two longer. Eat with a salad or on toast.

COTTAGE POTATOES

Imperial (Metric)	American
1 or 2 potatoes	1 or 2 potatoes
Seasoning to taste	Seasoning to taste
Chopped chives	Chopped chives
2 oz (50g) cottage cheese	1/4 cupful cottage cheese

1. Wash and prick the potatoes, then cook them in a medium oven for about an hour, or until soft to touch.

2. When ready, split the top of the potato, spread it open, and add the seasoning and chives and the cottage cheese. This is nice with a celery, apple and nut salad.

Note: This dish is a good choice when you're already using the oven, perhaps to do the week's baking. The cottage cheese is high in protein, low in calories, and gives a creamy taste to the drier potato. You can top jacket potatoes with all sorts of things — whatever you have handy in fact. Try left-over vegetables topped with a little butter, or add a tablespoonful of *dhall* (page 84). Lightly fried onions and walnuts make an unusual crunchy topping too.

WHEATGERM PATTIES

Imperial (Metric)
2-3 oz (50-75g) cooked beans (any kind you have handy)
½ small onion, finely chopped
1 small egg, beaten
Herbs and seasoning to taste
Wheatgerm to mix
2 tablespoonsful vegetable oil

American
⅓ cupful cooked beans (any kind you have handy)
½ small onion, finely chopped
1 small egg, beaten
Herbs and seasoning to taste
Wheatgerm to mix
2½ tablespoonsful vegetable oil

1. Mash the cooked beans, then combine them with the onion.

2. Beat the egg and add it to the beans with the herbs, seasoning, and enough wheatgerm to make a stiff dough.

3. Shape the dough into patties, dip them in some more wheatgerm, and shallow-fry them until brown on both sides.

HOT RICE-STUFFED TOMATOES

Illustrated in colour

Imperial (Metric)	American
2 large tomatoes	2 large tomatoes
½ oz (15g) polyunsaturated margarine	1 tablespoonful polyunsaturated margarine
1-2 oz (25-50g) mushrooms, finely chopped	½-¾ cupful finely chopped mushrooms
2 oz (50g) cooked brown rice	⅓ cupful cooked brown rice
1 oz (25g) cheese, grated	⅓ cupful grated cheese
Seasoning to taste	Seasoning to taste
1 tablespoonful tomato purée	1 tablespoonful tomato purée
Chives, chopped	Chives, chopped

1. Wash and dry the tomatoes. Cut a slice from the round end, scoop out the seeds and pulp and chop them coarsely.

2. Melt the margarine and *sauté* the mushrooms, then stir in the drained rice, tomato pulp, grated cheese and seasoning.

3. Add enough tomato *purée* to moisten and mix it in well.

4. Divide the mixture between each of the prepared tomato cases and arrange them in a shallow ovenproof dish, then cover each one with its own lid.

5. Bake at 375°F/190°C (Gas Mark 5) for about 10 minutes, or until the tomatoes are puffed up and hot right through. Serve at once sprinkled with chives.

Note: Any left-over grain can be used instead of the rice, as may oats or even breadcrumbs.

DEEP-FRIED CHEESE CUBES

Imperial (Metric)
3 oz (75g) mozzarella cheese
Plain wholemeal flour
Seasoning to taste
1 egg, beaten
2 oz (50g) dried wholemeal
  breadcrumbs
Vegetable oil for frying

American
¾ cupful mozzarella cheese
Plain wholemeal flour
Seasoning to taste
1 egg, beaten
1 cupful dried wholemeal
  breadcrumbs
Vegetable oil for frying

1. Cut the cheese into 1 in. cubes, then coat them lightly in flour which has been seasoned generously.

2. Dip the cubes into the beaten egg, then into the breadcrumbs and repeat the process.

3. Heat the oil and fry the cubes for just a few minutes until they are golden and crisp on the outside and creamy inside. Eaten with a crunchy green salad, this makes a very satisfying light lunch.

Note: If you prefer, you can cook various other cheeses in the same manner, but mozzarella is particularly suitable.

ONIONS ALMONDINE

Imperial (Metric)	American
1 large onion, sliced	1 large onion, sliced
1 oz (25g) polyunsaturated margarine or butter	2½ tablespoonsful polyunsaturated margarine or butter
1 teaspoonful vegetable oil	1 teaspoonful vegetable oil
1 tablespoonful honey	1 tablespoonful honey
1 oz (25g) split almonds	¼ cupful split almonds
Seasoning to taste	Seasoning to taste

1. Fry the onion gently in the combined margarine and oil.

2. When the onion begins to colour, add the honey, nuts and seasoning, and cook it gently for 5 minutes more, or until the onion is ready to eat. (Watch to make sure it doesn't burn.)

Note: The onions may be served on wholemeal toast for a quick lunch. If you have a spoonful of left-over cooked peas handy, add them to the mixture for extra protein and colour.

SHEPHERD'S PIE

Imperial (Metric)	American
4 oz (100g) lentils, split peas or soya minced 'meat', pre-soaked	½ cupful lentils, split peas or soya minced 'meat', pre-soaked
1 lb (½ kilo) potatoes	1 lb potatoes
1 tablespoonful vegetable oil	1 tablespoonful vegetable oil
1 onion, chopped	1 onion, chopped
2 tablespoonsful tomato purée	2½ tablespoonsful tomato purée
1 tablespoonful marjoram	1 tablespoonful marjoram
Seasoning to taste	Seasoning to taste
Polyunsaturated margarine or butter (optional)	Polyunsaturated margarine or butter (optional)

1. Cook the lentils, peas or soya minced meat in plenty of water until just tender.

2. Meanwhile, peel and cube the potatoes and steam them until soft.

3. In a frying pan, heat the oil and lightly *sauté* the onion.

4. Add the drained lentils, peas or soya meat together with the tomato *purée*, marjoram and seasoning. Cook for just a few minutes, stirring well so that the flavours mingle.

5. Spread the drained mixture across the base of a shallow ovenproof dish.

6. Mash the potatoes with a little sea salt and freshly ground black pepper, and spread them over the other ingredients. Use a fork to smooth the top and make a decorative pattern — for a more golden top, add a few knobs of margarine or butter.

7. If all the ingredients are hot, you can just heat the dish under the grill for a few minutes, or until the potatoes begin to colour. If cold, put the dish in the oven at 400°F/200°C (Gas Mark 6) for 10 minutes, or until heated through.

Note: This makes a very generous portion, probably enough for two or three helpings, but it is hardly worth making with fewer ingredients. Any left-over pie will keep and can be reheated another day. A much quicker way to make this dish, of course, is to use left-overs. Any protein and vegetable mix can be used as the base — just add a few herbs and some yeast extract or tomato *purée* if it needs more flavour (and if you cook extra potatoes, you'll always have some handy for the topping).

SWEET TREATS

It is always assumed that children have a sweet tooth, yet rarely admitted that sweet foods are popular with most people of all ages. The British are the world's leading consumers of sweets and chocolates. Ice cream parlours are springing up in High Streets across the country — despite our weather! Cake shops laden with goodies early in the day are invariably empty even before closing time. Whatever doctors and dietitians might say, sweet foods are — and will surely stay — a major part of our national diet.

If you wish to build good health, you should cut such foods to a minimum — most of them have nothing more to offer you than a tempting taste. Try to get used to having less sugar in your food and drinks, and *no* sugary between-meal snacks, and you will soon lose — or at least diminish — that sweet tooth.

Healthy Desserts
Finishing a meal with something sweet is, however, a tradition you may find hard to break. Tasty, healthy desserts are, of course, possible, but they usually require time and effort to prepare. If you are dining at home, that is fine. But when you are taking a packed lunch, you rarely have time for anything complicated. Besides, it would be difficult to transport.

The obvious sweet finale is fresh fruit. It is easy to carry, ready-wrapped in its own skin, and full of natural sugars. Yogurt is another favourite, although plain yogurt sweetened with honey or fruit *purée* is preferable to the flavoured (and over-sweetened) kind.

But there are many ways to round off your packed lunch without resorting to chocolate bars. Look through the recipes that follow. You will notice they are based on high-energy, high-nutrition ingredients such as dried fruit, nuts and honey. Usually they are quite simple to prepare in advance. And with the aid of clingfoil, or an individual-portion sized plastic container, they can be taken to work with the minimum of inconvenience to you, or damage to them! You may well find them so tasty you'll start serving them at home, too.

DATE 'FUDGE'

Imperial (Metric)	American
4 oz (100g) dates	¾ cupful dates
4 teaspoonsful lemon juice	4 teaspoonsful lemon juice
¼ pint (150ml) water	⅔ cupful water
2 oz (50g) polyunsaturated margarine	¼ cupful polyunsaturated margarine
2 oz (50g) wholemeal flour	½ cupful wholemeal flour

1. Chop the dates and put them into a saucepan with the lemon juice and water. Boil them for about 5 minutes, then mash them to make a thick *purée*.

2. Melt the margarine and add the flour, frying it gently for a few minutes.

3. Combine all the ingredients well, making sure there are no lumps.

4. Place the mixture in a shallow dish or tin, flatten it and leave it to cool.

5. Cut the 'fudge' into bite-sized pieces, store somewhere cold, and eat it within a few days.

Note: For variety, add some broken nuts, desiccated coconut, chopped crystallized ginger, or a few drops of pure vanilla essence.

CRUNCHY APPLE PURÉE

Imperial (Metric)	American
1 lb (½ kilo) cooking apples	1 lb cooking apples
¼ pint (150ml) water	⅔ cupful water
1 tablespoonful raw cane sugar	1 tablespoonful raw cane sugar
Pinch of mixed spice	Pinch of mixed spice
2 oz (50g) polyunsaturated margarine	¼ cupful polyunsaturated margarine
2 tablespoonsful honey	2½ tablespoonsful honey
2 oz (50g) oats	½ cupful rolled oats
1 oz (25g) walnuts, chopped (optional)	¼ cupful English walnuts, chopped (optional)

1. Core, slice and cook the apples with the water, sugar and spice to make a soft *purée*.

2. Melt the margarine and honey, stir them together well, then add the oats and continue cooking them for a few minutes longer. Set the mixture aside to cool.

3. In a small plastic container, layer the ingredients, adding a sprinkling of nuts (if using them). Finish with a layer of oats mixture and seal the container.

Note: The amounts given should make two good portions which will keep for a few days in the refrigerator (although the longer it is kept, the less crunchy it will be).

PEANUT BRITTLE

Imperial (Metric)
½ lb (¼ kilo) raw cane sugar
½ pint (¼ litre) water
1 teaspoonful lemon juice
1 lb (½ kilo) roasted peanuts

American
1⅓ cupsful raw cane sugar
1⅓ cupsful water
1 teaspoonful lemon juice
3 cupsful roasted peanuts

1. Place the sugar and water in a saucepan and stir it over a steady heat until the sugar dissolves.

2. Bring the mixture to the boil and cook it steadily until the mixture reaches the firm ball stage. (To test, drop a small quantity in a bowl of cold water — it should be pliable but firm.)

3. Add the lemon juice and then the nuts and continue cooking until, when tested in cold water, the sugar mixture breaks quite easily between your fingers.

4. Turn the mixture onto a greased board and, with hands dipped in cold water, break and roll it into balls. Alternatively, pour the mixture into a well greased tin and mark it into squares as it begins to set, then break it when completely set. Store the peanut brittle in a tin.

SWEET RICE CREAM

Imperial (Metric)
2 oz (50g) sultanas or raisins
4 oz (100g) cooked brown rice
A little milk

American
⅓ cupful golden seedless raisins or raisins
⅔ cupful cooked brown rice
A little milk

1. Plump the dried fruit in water first, then drain it well.

2. Put the rice and dried fruit into a blender and make it into a smooth cream. (Add a little milk if the mixture seems too dry.)

3. Place the mixture in a small plastic container and seal it.

APRICOT SURPRISE

Imperial (Metric)	American
4 oz (100g) dried apricot pieces	½ cupful dried apricot pieces
1 teaspoonful finely grated orange peel	1 teaspoonful finely grated orange peel
1-2 teaspoonsful ground cardamom (or powder)	1-2 teaspoonsful ground cardamom (or powder)
Desiccated coconut	Desiccated coconut

1. Wash the apricots, then soak them until plump. Cut them into pieces and mash them together with the peel and cardamom.

2. Shape the mixture into balls and roll them in the coconut. Wrap the balls in clingfilm.

Note: This is a quick and easy-to-make dessert with a very unusual taste.

LITTLE CHEESECAKES

Imperial (Metric)	American
1 oz (25g) cream cheese	2½ tablespoonsful cream cheese
1 oz (25g) natural yogurt	2½ tablespoonsful natural yogurt
1 teaspoonful honey	1 teaspoonful honey
½ oz (15g) raisins	1 tablespoonful raisins
4 wholewheat digestive biscuits	4 Graham crackers

1. Mix together the cream cheese, yogurt and honey until soft and well blended.

2. Stir in the raisins, then divide the mixture into two and sandwich each portion between two biscuits.

3. Wrap each 'cake' in clingfilm and place them in the refrigerator overnight. (If taken as part of a packed lunch, make sure your 'cake' is well protected as it will break apart if treated roughly.)

7. Try savoury Cheese Scones (page 117) as a summertime snack.

8. Bring a touch of romance to lunchtime with exotic Russian Fruit Salad (page 101).

CAROB NUT BALLS

Imperial (Metric)
4 oz (100g) peanut butter
3 tablespoonsful desiccated coconut
or skimmed milk powder
2 oz (50g) dates, finely chopped
2 oz (50g) sultanas, finely
chopped
Fruit juice to mix
Carob powder

American
1 cupful peanut butter
3½ tablespoonsful desiccated
coconut or skimmed milk powder
¼ cupful finely chopped dates
⅓ cupful golden seedless raisins,
finely chopped
Fruit juice to mix
Carob powder

1. Blend the peanut butter until smooth, then add the coconut or milk powder followed by the dried fruit.

2. Combine the ingredients well, adjusting the consistency of the mixture — if it is too wet, add more milk powder or coconut, if too dry, add a little fruit juice.

3. Shape the mixture into small balls and roll them firmly in carob powder. Wrap the balls in clingfilm and keep them in the refrigerator.

Note: These exotic-tasting sweets are very high in both protein and natural sugars. They are also high in calories, so if you intend to finish your lunch with one or two Carob Nut Balls, make sure you start it with something light and low in calories, such as a salad or fresh vegetable soup!

MUESLI

Imperial (Metric)	American
1 apple	1 apple
Squeeze of lemon juice	Squeeze of lemon juice
1 oz (25g) rolled oats	¼ cupful rolled oats
1 oz (25g) raisins or sultanas	2½ tablespoonsful raisins or golden seedless raisins
1 oz (25g) nuts, chopped	¼ cupful chopped nuts
1 oz (25g) wheatgerm (optional)	¼ cupful wheatgerm (optional)
2 oz (50g) skimmed milk powder	⅔ cupful skimmed milk powder

1. Core, then grate the apple into a bowl and mix it well in the lemon juice.

2. Stir together all the remaining ingredients and add them to the apple.

3. Place the muesli in a small container and seal it.

Note: Take your muesli with you this way, and when ready to eat it, simply add a little water (the milk powder will dissolve and make your muesli as creamy as if you'd added fresh milk).

This is a traditional recipe for muesli, but you can, of course, adapt it by varying the ingredients. Try some of the ideas given below — then try some of your own!

Vary the base with wheat, barley, rye and millet flakes (packets of mixed cereal for use as a muesli base can often be bought at health food shops). Vary the nuts, try them roasted instead of raw, add a few sunflower or pumpkin seeds or some desiccated coconut. Grind the nuts so that they're easier to digest. Try different dried fruits — prunes, dates, apples, pears, apricots, currants, bananas — all finely chopped. Add different fresh fruits instead of the apple, or together with it: strawberries, raspberries, gooseberries, orange, pear, banana, plums, peaches, apricots — whatever is in season. Different milks change the flavour, too. Add powdered soya milk, or a few spoonsful of cream or yogurt. Eliminate the milk and moisten with fruit juice instead.

If you like a sweeter dish, add some raw cane sugar or honey to taste, and for a really unusual muesli, grate a young, sweet carrot and add it to the mixture — delicious!

BANANA CREAM

Imperial (Metric)
1 ripe banana
Squeeze of lemon juice
1 tablespoonful honey
4 tablespoonsful soured cream

American
1 ripe banana
Squeeze of lemon juice
1 tablespoonful honey
5 tablespoonsful soured cream

1. Mash the banana until creamy, add the lemon juice to keep it from browning.

2. Stir in the honey and then the soured cream.

3. Place the mixture in a small plastic container, seal it, and keep it as cool as possible until needed. This tastes nice accompanied by crispy biscuits such as Oaties or Nutty Shortbread (pages 111 and 112).

Note: This is one dessert that really should be made on the morning of the day you intend to eat it.

DRIED FRUIT AND NUT NIBBLE

Imperial (Metric)	American
4 oz (100g) cashew nuts, broken	¾ cupful broken cashew nuts
4 oz (100g) sunflower seeds	1 cupful sunflower seeds
4 oz (100g) flaked almonds	1 cupful flaked almonds
4 oz (100g) currants	⅔ cupful currants
4 oz (100g) dried pears, chopped	½ cupful chopped dried pears
4 oz (100g) raisins	⅔ cupful raisins
4 oz (100g) desiccated coconut	1⅓ cupsful desiccated coconut

1. Simply combine all the ingredients well, and keep the mixture
   handy in a sealed jar to pick at whenever you fancy nibbling
   something that's as healthy as it is tasty.

Note: You can try other nuts and other fruits, changing the
quantities so that you use more of a particular favourite; and roasted
rather than raw nuts make a pleasant change too.

SESAME SQUARES

Imperial (Metric)	American
4 oz (100g) sesame seeds	⅔ cupful sesame seeds
4 tablespoonsful honey	5 tablespoonsful honey
Soya flour to mix	Soya flour to mix

1. Stir the seeds into the honey, then add enough of the soya flour
   to make the mixture firm.

2. Turn the mixture into a shallow greased tin and smooth the top.
   Set it aside in the refrigerator.

Note: Eaten within a day or so, it will be rather like fudge, but if you
can manage to resist it a little longer, the mixture will harden to a
delicious sweet-like confection, which should be cut into squares.

RUSSIAN FRUIT SALAD
Illustrated in colour

Imperial (Metric)	American
1 oz (25g) dark cherries or grapes	2½ tablespoonsful dark cherries or grapes
1 oz (25g) red or black currants	¼ cupful red or black currants
1 red plum	1 red plum
1 oz (25g) raspberries	¼ cupful raspberries
1-2 tablespoonsful pure black currant juice	1-2½ tablespoonsful pure black currant juice

1. Mix together all the fruit, then leave it to marinate in the black currant juice.

Note: Take this to work in a plastic container, or small screw-top jar. If you can leave it somewhere cool at work, it's worth making up two days' supply.

This dark and dramatic-looking fruit salad has a sharp taste which is very refreshing. It will also provide you with a good supply of vitamin C. For variety, or to make the taste less sharp, swirl in a tablespoonful of cream or plain yogurt just before you eat your fruit salad.

STUFFED DATES

Imperial (Metric)	American
6-8 whole dates	6-8 whole dates
1 oz (25g) cream cheese	2½ tablespoonsful cream cheese
3-4 whole Brazil nuts	3-4 whole Brazil nuts

1. Stone the dates carefully. Stuff half of them with a small portion of cream cheese, and the others with a brazil nut each.

2. Alternatively, chop the nuts, mix them into the cream cheese, and use this mixture to fill all the dates.

3. Pack them firmly in a small container or wrap a few together in clingfilm.

ALMOND ORANGE AMBROSIA

Imperial (Metric)	American
1 large orange	1 large orange
1 oz (25g) sliced almonds, raw or roasted	¼ cupful sliced almonds, raw or roasted
½-1 oz (15-25g) raw cane sugar	1-2½ tablespoonsful raw cane sugar
Pure orange juice	Pure orange juice

1. Slice the orange finely and form layers, with the nuts and half of the sugar, in a small plastic container.

2. Sprinkle the remaining sugar over the top and pour in enough orange juice to moisten the fruit. Seal the container and chill the mixture. (Ambrosia tastes best when it has been left overnight.)

FIG BARS

Imperial (Metric)	American
4 oz (100g) dried figs	½ cupful dried figs
4 oz (100g) sesame or sunflower seeds	⅔ cupful sesame or sunflower seeds
Rice paper	Rice paper

1. Wash and dry the figs, then chop them into small pieces. Place the figs in a bowl and mash them until a thick paste is formed.

2. Mix in the seeds, distributing them evenly.

3. Sandwich the paste between two sheets of rice paper and cut out bars.

4. Wrap each bar in clingfilm and keep them somewhere cool until needed.

OAT CRUNCH CEREAL

Imperial (Metric)	American
4 tablespoonsful honey	5 tablespoonsful honey
8 tablespoonsful vegetable oil	10 tablespoonsful vegetable oil
1 lb (½ kilo) rolled oats	4 cupsful rolled oats
4 oz (100g) desiccated coconut	1⅓ cupsful desiccated coconut
4 oz (100g) raisins	⅔ cupful raisins
4 oz (100g) roasted peanuts	¾ cupful roasted peanuts

1. Combine the honey and oil, and pour the mixture into a large baking tray.

2. Add the oats and coconut, stirring to make sure they are covered in the oil mixture.

3. Bake the mixture in a slow oven for an hour or so, until the oats turn golden and are crisp to touch. (You may need to stir the ingredients every now and again to cook them evenly.)

4. Mix in the raisins and peanuts, and leave the mixture to cool. Store in a jar and use as necessary.

Note: Make your Oat Crunch Cereal this way only if your oven is already in use. Alternatively, cook it in a large frying pan on the top of the cooker — use a low heat and stir it frequently.

This inexpensive cereal can be eaten with milk or cream. Alternatively, sprinkle it over fruit, stir it into yogurt, or add it to smooth desserts (such as Banana Cream) for a contrast in textures. You can also eat it, as a nutrition-packed nibble, straight from the jar.

APRICOT GINGER CRUNCH BARS

Imperial (Metric)
½ lb (¼ kilo) ginger biscuits
  (made with wholemeal flour)
2 oz (50g) polyunsaturated
  margarine
2 tablespoonsful honey
4 oz (100g) dried apricot pieces,
  chopped

American
½ lb ginger biscuits (made with
  wholemeal flour)
¼ cupful polyunsaturated
  margarine
2½ tablespoonsful honey
½ cupful dried apricot pieces,
  chopped

1. Crush the biscuits into small but uneven pieces, then mix them well with the melted margarine.

2. Stir in the honey and chopped apricots.

3. When the mixture is thoroughly blended, transfer it to a small, shallow cake tin and press it down firmly, making sure it is evenly distributed.

4. Set the mixture aside to firm up and then cut it into bars.

Note: This recipe can be made using different dried fruits — whatever you have handy — a mixture can be interesting. A few chopped nuts make a tasty addition, or try a spoonful or two of desiccated coconut.

HONEYED APPLES

Imperial (Metric)
3 apples
3 tablespoonsful honey
Small pinch of cream of tartar

American
3 apples
3½ tablespoonsful honey
Small pinch of cream of tartar

1. Wash and dry the apples, then remove the stalks and push a wooden stick into the stalk end of each one.

2. In a heavy saucepan, heat the honey very gently until it begins to boil, then add the cream of tartar and stir well.

3. Continue boiling gently until a little of the mixture dropped into cold water immediately forms a firm ball that can still be moulded.

4. Dip each apple into the mixture and twist it to coat it completely.

5. Stand each apple in a cup, or lay them on a greased tray and leave them until cold.

Note: This is a particularly suitable sweet treat for youngsters, although grown-ups who have the courage to eat them in public will thoroughly enjoy them too!

TOFU MAPLE FRUIT WHIP

Imperial (Metric)
4 oz (100g) tofu
4 oz (100g) ripe fresh fruit, such as apricots, pear, black currants etc.
Maple syrup to taste
Oat Crunch Cereal (page 103) or a few nuts

American
²/₃ cupful tofu
1 cupful ripe fresh fruit, such as apricots, pear, black currants, etc.
Maple syrup to taste
Oat Crunch Cereal (page 103) or a few nuts

1. Just combine the first three ingredients and blend them until thick and creamy. (This is best done in a blender, but can also be done by hand.)

2. Spoon the mixture into a dish or small plastic container if it is to be eaten away from home, and keep it cool as long as possible.

3. Sprinkle some Oat Crunch Cereal or chopped nuts over the top if desired.

PEACH CONDÉ

Imperial (Metric)
1 oz (25g) brown rice
½ pint (¼ litre) milk
1 oz (25g) raw cane sugar
Knob of butter (optional)
¼ pint (150ml) pure orange or
  lemon juice
½ oz (15g) arrowroot
1 fresh peach

American
¼ cupful brown rice
1⅓ cupsful milk
2½ tablespoonsful raw cane sugar
Knob of butter (optional)
⅔ cupful pure orange or lemon
  juice
1 tablespoonful arrowroot
1 fresh peach

1. Place the rice and milk in a saucepan, bring the milk to the boil, then simmer the rice until it is tender and most of the milk has been absorbed.

2. Stir in the sugar and, if liked, a knob of butter to make it creamier.

3. When cool, divide the rice between two dishes or two small plastic containers.

4. Make the sauce by gently boiling the juice and arrowroot together for a few minutes until it thickens, then let it cool for a few minutes.

5. Halve and stone the peach, and place it cut-side down on top of the rice.

6. Pour a little of the sauce over the rice and fruit and leave it to set. (This sweet is best kept as cool as possible.)

Note: The ideal time to make peach *condé* is when you have some left-over rice.

LUNCH BOX BAKING

Because cakes and biscuits are seen as something of a treat, it is usually assumed they are bad for you. Usually, of course, they are. So that they will appeal to appetites jaded by too much over-refined food, they have become increasingly sweet, rich and fatty. The result is a non-food that contains little of benefit, but a lot that is harmful. White flour, refined sugar (in the form of jam, icing sugar and chocolate) cholesterol-rich cream — all add up to surplus weight, decaying teeth and bad digestion.

This does not mean that, in order to eat healthily, you have got to automatically give up cakes and biscuits. It is what *kind* you eat that matters. Buy them from a health food shop or, better still, bake them yourself. The nice thing about baking wholesome cakes is that they're far less fiddly than the other kind. Made with fresh, natural ingredients, they taste mouth-wateringly good just as they are. There is no need to ice them with this, fill them with that, add artificial flavourings and colouring. It is not imperative that they rise perfectly, colour evenly, or that they are eaten immediately before they go stale. Just throw your favourite ingredients into a bowl, mix and cook them — and enjoy.

Such baked goods can turn a lunch into a treat. Do your baking early in the week, and you will have something delicious to finish your meal with every day. If you are not feeling hungry, a piece of wholewheat cake and a cup of peppermint tea is the kind of snack that will give you energy for the afternoon, and then some!

The recipes given here have all been chosen for their 'packability'. None of them are exceptionally crumbly, sticky or flaky, and just need wrapping in foil if they're to be taken as part of a packed lunch. Anyone lunching at home will find them just as delicious! Should any of them get a little stale, try spreading them with butter, cream cheese, honey or nut butters.

APPLE TURNOVERS
Illustrated in colour

Imperial (Metric)

6 oz (150g) wholemeal shortcrust pastry (page 65)

2 large cooking apples

1 tablespoonful raw cane sugar

Mixed spice and cinnamon to taste

1 oz (25g) sultanas

American

1½ cupsful wholemeal shortcrust pastry (page 65)

2 large cooking apples

1 tablespoonful raw cane sugar

Mixed spice and cinnamon to taste

2½ tablespoonsful golden seedless raisins

1. Roll out the pastry and cut it into four squares.

2. Core the apples, then chop them roughly into cubes and divide them between the squares, adding a sprinkling of sugar, spice and sultanas.

3. Fold the pastry to make a triangle, brush the edges with a little water, and press them together with a fork.

4. Lift the turnovers gently onto a lightly greased baking sheet and bake them at 400°F/200°C (Gas Mark 6) for approximately 15-20 minutes.

GINGERBREAD

Imperial (Metric)	American
½ lb (¼ kilo) plain wholemeal flour	2 cupsful plain wholemeal flour
1 teaspoonful bicarbonate of soda	1 teaspoonful bicarbonate of soda
2 teaspoonsful ground ginger	2 teaspoonsful ground ginger
4 oz (100g) raw cane sugar	½ cupful raw cane sugar
4 oz (100g) polyunsaturated margarine	½ cupful polyunsaturated margarine
1 tablespoonful molasses	1 tablespoonful molasses
1 egg	1 egg
Milk to mix	Milk to mix

1. Sieve the dry ingredients into a bowl.

2. Place the margarine and molasses in a saucepan and heat them gently until melted.

3. Stir this mixture into the dry ingredients and beat in the egg and as much milk as necessary to make a thick batter.

4. Line a 7 in. square tin with greased greaseproof paper, and pour in the cake mixture.

5. Bake the cake in the centre of the oven for 15 minutes at 350°F/180°C (Gas Mark 4) then for a further 45 minutes at 325°F/170°C (Gas Mark 3). Test that the cake is cooked before removing it from the oven, then let it cool for 10 minutes before placing it on an airing tray.

Note: Gingerbread is a very good source of iron.

MARMALADE CAKE
Illustrated in colour

Imperial (Metric)

2 teaspoonsful baking powder
1/2 lb (1/4 kilo) plain wholemeal flour
6 oz (150g) polyunsaturated margarine
4 oz (100g) raw cane sugar
4 tablespoonsful pure orange or grapefruit juice
1 egg
2-3 tablespoonsful raw sugar marmalade
1 tablespoonful grated orange peel (optional)

American

2 teaspoonsful baking powder
2 cupsful plain wholemeal flour
3/4 cupful polyunsaturated margarine
1/2 cupful raw cane sugar
5 tablespoonsful pure orange or grapefruit juice
1 egg
2 1/2-3 1/2 tablespoonsful raw sugar marmalade
1 tablespoonful grated orange peel (optional)

1. Sieve the baking powder into the flour, then mix all the ingredients together, making sure they are well blended.

2. Turn the mixture into a greased loaf tin and bake the cake for about an hour at 350°F/180°C (Gas Mark 4).

Note: This is a cake that's quick to make and delicious to eat.

DATE FINGERS

Imperial (Metric)

4 oz (100g) dates, finely chopped
1/2 lb (1/4 kilo) rolled oats
3 oz (75g) raw cane sugar
5 oz (125g) polyunsaturated margarine

American

1/2 cupful finely chopped dates
2 cupsful rolled oats
1/3 cupful raw cane sugar
2/3 cupful polyunsaturated margarine

1. Combine the dates with the oats and sugar, making sure they are evenly distributed.

2. Warm the margarine until melted, then mix it in with dry ingredients.

3. Oil a Swiss roll tin (or similar) and spoon the mixture into it, pressing it down gently.

4. Bake at 375°F/190°C (Gas Mark 5) for 30 minutes. Mark the mixture into slices before it hardens, but do not remove them from the tin until cool.

NUTTY SHORTBREAD

Imperial (Metric)
½ lb (¼ kilo) polyunsaturated
  margarine
3 oz (75g) raw cane sugar
¾ lb (350g) plain wholemeal flour
3 oz (75g) roasted hazelnuts,
  chopped

American
1 cupful polyunsaturated
  margarine
⅓ cupful raw cane sugar
3 cupsful plain wholemeal flour
⅔ cupful roasted hazelnuts,
  chopped

1. Beat the margarine and sugar together until light and creamy.

2. Gradually add the flour and then the nuts (the mixture will be of a similar consistency to a crumble).

3. Press the mixture into a greased Swiss roll tin and bake on the middle shelf of the oven at 300°F/150°C (Gas Mark 2) for 30 minutes until golden.

4. Cut into slices whilst still hot, but leave the mixture to cool in the tin.

OATIES

Imperial (Metric)	American
4 oz (100g) plain wholemeal flour	1 cupful plain wholemeal flour
½ teaspoonful baking powder	½ teaspoonful baking powder
Pinch of sea salt	Pinch of sea salt
4 oz (100g) polyunsaturated margarine	½ cupful polyunsaturated margarine
4 oz (100g) raw cane sugar	½ cupful raw cane sugar
1 egg	1 egg
1 tablespoonful milk	1 tablespoonful milk
1 teaspoonful pure vanilla essence	1 teaspoonful pure vanilla essence
4 oz (100g) rolled oats	1 cupful rolled oats

1. Sift together the flour, baking powder and salt.

2. Beat the margarine and sugar together, then add the egg, milk and essence.

3. When well mixed add the flour gradually, and finally the oats.

4. Drop the mixture by the spoonful onto a greased baking sheet, leaving room for expansion.

5. Bake at 350°F/180°C (Gas Mark 4) for 10-15 minutes until lightly browned.

BANANA TEA CAKE

Illustrated in colour

Imperial (Metric)	American
2 oz (50g) polyunsaturated margarine	¼ cupful polyunsaturated margarine
4 oz (100g) raw cane sugar	½ cupful raw cane sugar
1 lb (½ kilo) ripe bananas, mashed	1 lb ripe bananas, mashed
7 oz (200g) plain wholemeal flour	1¾ cupsful plain wholemeal flour
¼ pint (150ml) warm water	⅔ cupful warm water
1 oz (25g) chopped peel (optional)	2½ tablespoonsful chopped peel (optional)
1 oz (25g) chopped walnuts (optional)	¼ cupful chopped English walnuts (optional)

1. Melt the margarine, add the sugar and then the mashed banana.

2. Stir in the flour and add enough water to make the mixture fairly stiff.

3. Add the peel and walnuts, distributing them as evenly as possible.

4. Bake the cake in a greased tin at 350°F/180°C (Gas Mark 4) for 45 minutes to an hour.

COCONUT BREAD

Imperial (Metric)
½ lb (¼ kilo) plain wholemeal flour
4 oz (100g) desiccated coconut
1 tablespoonful baking powder
½ teaspoonful bicarbonate of soda
Pinch of sea salt
2 eggs
4 tablespoonsful honey
8 tablespoonsful vegetable oil
1 teaspoonful pure almond essence
Squeeze of lemon juice
¼ pint (150ml) milk

American
2 cupsful plain wholemeal flour
1⅓ cupsful desiccated coconut
1 tablespoonful baking powder
½ teaspoonful bicarbonate of soda
Pinch of sea salt
2 eggs
5 tablespoonsful honey
10 tablespoonsful vegetable oil
1 teaspoonful pure almond essence
Squeeze of lemon juice
⅔ cupful milk

1. Place all the dry ingredients in a bowl and stir them well.

2. In a separate bowl, beat the eggs, add the honey, oil, essence and lemon juice.

3. Add the milk and combine the wet mixture with the flour. (The dough should be stiff.)

4. Place the mixture in a greased tin and bake at 350°F/180°C (Gas Mark 4) for about 30 minutes. (Eat this bread on its own, with butter, honey, date spread or nut butter.)

SUNSHINE BISCUITS

Imperial (Metric)	American
½ lb (¼ kilo) sunflower seeds	2 cupsful sunflower seeds
6 oz (150g) plain wholemeal flour	1½ cupsful plain wholemeal flour
1 egg	1 egg
2 tablespoonsful honey	2½ tablespoonsful honey
2 tablespoonsful vegetable oil	2½ tablespoonsful vegetable oil
A little water	A little water

1. Grind the seeds in a grinder to make a fine meal, then mix it well with the flour.

2. Beat the egg and combine it with honey and oil, then stir this mixture into the dry ingredients with enough water to make a firm dough.

3. With floured hands, split the dough into three sections, shape each one into a roll of two inches wide, wrap them in foil and leave them in the fridge for a few hours. (When cool, the rolls can more easily be sliced into ½ in. rounds.)

4. Place the rounds on a greased baking sheet and cook them for 20 minutes at 350°F/180°C (Gas Mark 4) or until they are just turning golden.

Note: Sunflower seeds are expensive (they're also packed with goodness!) so don't let the unusual taste tempt you to eat too many Sunshine Biscuits at one go!

FRUIT AND BRAN LOAF

Imperial (Metric)	American
4 oz (100g) All-Bran	1½ cupsful All-Bran
3 oz (75g) raw cane sugar	⅓ cupful raw cane sugar
4 oz (100g) mixed dried fruit	⅔ cupful mixed dried fruit
½ pint (¼ litre) milk	1⅓ cupsful milk
6 oz (150g) plain wholemeal flour	1½ cupsful plain wholemeal flour
2 teaspoonsful baking powder	2 teaspoonsful baking powder

1. Soak the *All Bran,* sugar and mixed fruit in the milk for an hour.

2. Mix together the flour and baking powder, then add them to the other ingredients. (The mixture should be quite moist.)

3. Spoon the mixture into a greased tin and bake the cake at 350°F/180°C (Gas Mark 4) for about an hour.

PEANUT CRISPS

Imperial (Metric)	American
4 oz (100g) plain wholemeal flour	1 cupful plain wholemeal flour
2 teaspoonsful baking powder	2 teaspoonsful baking powder
1½ oz (40g) polyunsaturated margarine	3½ tablespoonsful polyunsaturated margarine
3 oz (75g) raw cane sugar	⅓ cupful raw cane sugar
1 egg	1 egg
2 oz (50g) peanuts, raw or lightly roasted	3½ tablespoonsful peanuts, raw or lightly roasted

1. Place the flour in a bowl with the baking powder, then add the fat and sugar.

2. Combine the ingredients well, then add the egg and chopped peanuts to make a stiff dough.

3. Grease a baking sheet and drop dough onto it in small rough heaps, leaving room for the mixture to spread.

4. Bake at 375°F/190°C (Gas Mark 5) for 15 minutes and allow the biscuits to cool a little before removing them from the sheet.

LEMON BISCUITS

Imperial (Metric)	American
½ lb (¼ kilo) plain wholemeal flour	2 cupsful plain wholemeal flour
4 oz (100g) polyunsaturated margarine	½ cupful polyunsaturated margarine
4 oz (100g) raw cane sugar	½ cupful raw cane sugar
Grated rind of 1 lemon	Grated rind of 1 lemon
Lemon juice and water (mixed)	Lemon juice and water (mixed)

1. Place the flour in a bowl, rub in the fat and then mix in the sugar and lemon rind.

2. Add just enough lemon juice and water to make a soft dough.

3. Roll out the dough on a floured board to about ¼ in. thick, cut it into rounds and place them on a greased baking sheet.

4. Bake at 350°F/180°C (Gas Mark 4) for 20-30 minutes.

Note: You can vary the flavour of these quick-to-make biscuits by replacing the lemon rind with orange rind or currants.

APRICOT HONEY SLICES

Imperial (Metric)	American
½ lb (¼ kilo) dried apricot halves (or pieces)	1½ cupsful dried apricot halves (or pieces)
3 oz (75g) polyunsaturated margarine	⅓ cupful polyunsaturated margarine
6 oz (150g) plain wholemeal flour	1½ cupsful plain wholemeal flour
2 oz (50g) raw cane sugar	¼ cupful raw cane sugar
Milk to mix	Milk to mix
2 tablespoonsful honey	2½ tablespoonsful honey

1. Soak the apricots overnight, then cook them gently.

2. Rub the margarine into the flour, then add the sugar and enough milk to bind the mixture to a smooth dough.

3. Divide the dough and roll it into two thin sheets, then place one in a greased Swiss roll tin.

4. Melt the honey and add the dried apricots, then spread them over the pastry base.

5. Cover the apricots with the second sheet of pastry and brush with a little milk.

6. Bake at 350°F/180°C (Gas Mark 4) for 30 minutes, then cut into slices when cold.

CHEESE SCONES
Illustrated in colour

Imperial (Metric)	American
½ lb (¼ kilo) self-raising wholemeal flour	2 cupsful self-raising wholemeal flour
Pinch each of sea salt and cayenne pepper	Pinch each of sea salt and cayenne pepper
1 oz (25g) polyunsaturated margarine	2½ tablespoonsful polyunsaturated margarine
2 oz (50g) Cheddar cheese, finely grated	½ cupful finely grated Cheddar cheese
Milk to mix	Milk to mix

1. Sieve the flour and seasoning into a bowl.

2. Rub in the margarine and cheese and enough milk to form a stiff dough.

3. Turn the dough onto a floured board, knead it lightly, then roll it out to ½-¾ in. thickness and cut it into rounds 2 in. wide.

4. Place the scones on a greased baking sheet and bake them at 425°F/220°C (Gas Mark 7) for about 15 minutes or until firm to touch.

SESAME STRIPS

Imperial (Metric)
4 oz (100g) polyunsaturated
  margarine
4 oz (100g) sesame seeds
¼ pint (150ml) milk
½ lb (¼ kilo) plain wholemeal flour
Sea salt and herbs to taste

American
½ cupful polyunsaturated
  margarine
⅔ cupful sesame seeds
⅔ cupful milk
2 cupsful plain wholemeal flour
Sea salt and herbs to taste

1. Blend together all the ingredients using sufficient flour to make a firm dough.

2. On a floured board, roll the dough out as thinly as possible, then cut it into strips and place them on a greased baking sheet.

3. Cook at 375°F/190°C (Gas Mark 5) for 15 minutes, then leave them to cool and store the strips in a tin.

CAROB WALNUT SQUARES

Imperial (Metric)	**American**
4 oz (100g) polyunsaturated margarine	½ cupful polyunsaturated margarine
4 oz (100g) raw cane sugar	½ cupful raw cane sugar
2 eggs, lightly beaten	2 eggs, lightly beaten
4 oz (100g) self-raising wholemeal flour	1 cupful self-raising wholemeal flour
2 oz (50g) carob powder	½ cupful carob powder
Pinch of sea salt	Pinch of sea salt
1-2 oz (25-50g) walnut pieces	¼-½ cupful English walnut pieces

1. Beat the margarine until creamy and blend it well with the sugar.

2. Stir in the eggs, then add the flour, carob powder and salt, making sure all the ingredients are thoroughly blended.

3. Grease and flour a shallow square or oblong tin and shake off the excess flour.

4. Spoon in the cake mixture and spread the top evenly before scattering the walnut pieces over the top.

5. Bake at 350°F/180°C (Gas Mark 4) for 20-25 minutes, or until it feels firm when pressed lightly with the finger-tips.

6. Leave the cake to cool completely before cutting it into squares.

CHERRY CHEESECAKE

For crust:

Imperial (Metric)	American
½ lb (¼ kilo) wholemeal digestive biscuits	2 cupsful crushed Graham crackers
3 oz (75g) polyunsaturated margarine or butter, melted	7½ tablespoonsful polyunsaturated margarine or butter, melted
1 oz (25g) raw cane sugar	2½ tablespoonsful raw cane sugar

For filling:

Imperial (Metric)	American
2 eggs	2 eggs
3 oz (75g) raw cane sugar	⅓ cupful raw cane sugar
½ lb (¼ kilo) cottage cheese, sieved	1 cupful cottage cheese, sieved
¼ pint (150ml) soured cream	⅔ cupful soured cream
1 oz (25g) wholemeal flour	¼ cupful wholemeal flour
Squeeze of lemon juice	Squeeze of lemon juice
3 tablespoonsful raw sugar cherry jam	3½ tablespoonsful raw sugar cherry jam

1. To make the crust, crush the biscuits into fine crumbs and mix them with margarine and sugar.

2. Press the mixture firmly and evenly against the base and sides of an 8-9 in. flan dish or flan ring placed on an ovenproof plate.

3. Bake the crust at 375°F/190°C (Gas Mark 5), then allow it to cool before adding the filling.

4. Beat together the eggs and sugar, add the cottage cheese and cream with the flour and lemon juice and mix them well.

5. Spread the cherry jam across the base of the flan crust, then carefully spoon in the cheese mixture and smooth the top.

6. Bake at 325°F/170°C (Gas Mark 3) for 45-50 minutes or until firm.

Note. Using cherry jam in this way makes it quick and easy to add extra interest to your cheesecake — it also makes it easier to carry if you eat lunch away from home. Traditionally, however, this cheesecake would be cooked without the jam and served, instead, with a sauce spread over the top. A good one can be made by bringing to the boil the contents of a medium-sized tin of cherries in their own juice with ¼ pint (150ml) of water and 1 tablespoonful of arrowroot. Simmer the mixture for a minute or so until it thickens, then leave it to cool before spreading it over the top of the cheesecake.

SPICED HONEY CAKE

Imperial (Metric)
5 oz (125g) polyunsaturated
  margarine or butter
5 oz (125g) raw cane sugar
5 tablespoonsful clear honey
1 tablespoonful water
2 eggs
7 oz (200g) self-raising wholemeal
  flour
1 teaspoonful mixed spice
Pinch of sea salt
2 oz (50g) candied peel
2 oz (50g) flaked almonds

American
²/₃ cupful polyunsaturated
  margarine or butter
²/₃ cupful raw cane sugar
6 tablespoonsful clear honey
1 tablespoonful water
2 eggs
1³/₄ cupsful self-raising wholemeal
  flour
1 teaspoonful mixed spice
Pinch of sea salt
¹/₃ cupful candied peel
¹/₂ cupful flaked almonds

1. In a saucepan, and over a low heat, combine the margarine, sugar, honey and water, stirring continually until the mixture is well blended.

2. Set the mixture aside to cool slightly, then beat in the eggs.

3. Sift together the flour and spices and salt and add them to the other ingredients, beating until the mixture is thick and smooth.

4. Stir in the chopped peel and spoon the mixture into a shallow 10 by 8 in. tin, first greasing and lining it with silver foil. Sprinkle the almonds over the top.

5. Bake the cake at 350°F/180°C (Gas Mark 4) for 30-35 minutes, or until the cake has risen and is firm to touch. Leave it to cool for a few minutes before transferring it to a wire rack and do not cut it into squares until completely cold.

YOUR HEALTHY EATING PLAN

The prospect of having to think up menus for, and then prepare, five or so packed lunches a week probably seems more daunting than it need be. Once you get into the habit of taking packed lunches you'll wonder why you never bothered before.

Planning in advance is vital if you are going to provide enough variety to keep your lunches interesting, satisfying, and nutritionally sound. Have in mind at least a rough idea of what you intend to take for lunch through the week, then when you do your weekly food shopping, buy for your lunches as well. As has been suggested, you can often save time by preparing and cooking your lunch snack along with your evening meal. Baking can be done, say once a week, and a variety of sweets can be made up in a batch and kept somewhere cool until needed. You can also, of course, freeze many savoury dishes, breads and cakes; so if you have a freezer it is well worth cooking in bulk, and simply defrosting when you run out.

Packaging

Battered sandwiches, soggy salads, and crummy cakes are the end result of bad packaging. There is no point in preparing a delicious snack if, by the time you are ready to eat it, it is barely recognizable. Nowadays you can buy a variety of lightweight containers, all shapes and sizes, so do not be tempted to stuff everything into a paper bag and hope it is going to stay whole and wholesome — because it won't. One medium-sized oblong shaped container will take sandwiches or salad, flans, cold vegetables, fruit *compote*, cake, — just about anything. So a few pennies will save you wasting food, time and energy.

Alternatively, an even more economy-conscious idea is to re-use containers in which you have purchased something else. So many foods now come in neat, light, plastic packs, and most have lids that can be used time and again. If not, however, use the base and cover it with clingfoil, preferably secured with an elastic band to keep your lunch completely airtight and protected. Make a habit of collecting such containers and pots — then you will always have the right one for whatever it is you want to carry.

Another valuable item is one of those individual-sized Thermos flasks that can now be found in most shops. It can be used to take hot soups in winter, cold soups or drinks in summer, and is slim enough to slip into a bag without weighing you down.

If you have facilities at work for storing one or two items, so much the better. Many of the people who are against packed lunches are put off by the prospect of eating out of a polythene box, or with a plastic fork. They like their meals to have a little more style! If you feel this way, keep a china plate, an attractive cup or mug, and a set of cutlery tucked away in a drawer somewhere. A salt and pepper cruet is nice to have handy, too.

You can also save yourself transporting items back and forth unnecessarily by keeping certain foods at work, and using them to supplement the fresh items you prepare each day. Crispbreads, biscuits, nut butters, some spreads, dried fruit, nuts, margarine — all will keep for a reasonable time in a cool spot.

Drinks

Drinking too much tea and/or coffee is a hazard for anyone who works away from home. Because having a drink provides an excuse for having a break, it is easy to down cup after cup and hardly notice you're doing so. Not only can this cause weight problems by providing excess fluid (as well as milk and sugar), but tea and coffee do little to build good health. The stimulants they contain may perk you up, but they also use up valuable energy, as well as inhibiting the body's use of various nutrients. If you would like to cut down on them, keep some decaffeinated coffee and herb teas at work, too. Providing you have access to hot water, you'll always be able to enjoy a 'decent' cup of tea or coffee with your lunch.

Sharing

Sharing is well worth considering if you work with someone who would also like to take packed lunches, and preferably who shares your tastes in food! One week you buy and prepare lunch for the two of you, the next week it is your friend's turn; or, of course, you can do it on a daily basis. This is also a useful way to cater for hungry children who do not, for one reason or another, have school meals. Work shared is worked halved, and you will probably find it makes your housekeeping go that bit further, too!

Menu Suggestions

Now you're all set to start making, taking and enjoying your packed lunches, here are some suggestions to get you going. They are based on the recipes in this book, and have been chosen to make your lunches as varied as possible. Once you have got the idea, be imaginative and get some more of your own. Treat the planning and preparing of your packed lunches, not as a task, but as something pleasant and rewarding.

Packed Lunches for Summer

MONDAY Cheese Savoury Slice, mixed salad. Almond orange ambrosia.

TUESDAY Brazilian Loaf, Ratatouille. Yogurt.

WEDNESDAY Bean sprout salad, Cheese Scone. Fruit *purée*.

THURSDAY Paella. Fresh fruit.

FRIDAY Egg *pâté*, carrot and celery sticks. Sesame Strips. Cake.

Packed Lunches for Winter

MONDAY Large slice Pizza. Fresh fruit.

TUESDAY Egg mayonnaise salad. Wheatgerm bread with apple butter.

WEDNESDAY Meal-in-a-Soup (in flask). Fig Bar.

THURSDAY Creamy Peas Pasty. Celery, tomato. Russian fruit salad.

FRIDAY Nut butter and cucumber sandwiches. Apricot Surprise.

Lunches at Home

For the housebound, the main problem is finding the will-power to
stop what you're doing, sit down, and eat lunch. There is no easy
answer to this — only the suggestion that once you have tried it for a
week or two, and discovered how much better and more energetic
you feel (for what really amounts to only a little extra effort) you'll
find you look forward to your lunch break.

Here are some ideas, all of which are reasonably quick and easy to
prepare. Do not forget that if a dish does require more time than
usual, like the soups for example, it is worth making double the
portion.

Summer Lunches

MONDAY Cheese and Onion Crispies, mixed salad. Banana
    Cream.

TUESDAY Mushrooms Paprika on Toast, celery sticks. Stuffed
    dates.

WEDNESDAY Protein Vegetable Drink, wholewheat crisp-
    breads. Fresh fruit.

THURSDAY Mixed salad with Tahini Dressing. Cake.

FRIDAY Cold Cauliflower and Potato Soup. Fruit salad with nuts.

Winter Lunches

MONDAY Eggburger on wholewheat bap. Fresh fruit.

TUESDAY Miso Soup, mixed salad with nuts. Biscuits.

WEDNESDAY Bean Hotpot. Yogurt.

THURSDAY Slimmer's Spaghetti. Dried fruit *compote*.

FRIDAY Salad sandwich. Hot 'Chocolate' drink.

Happy lunching, everyone!

INDEX